The Six Short Plays by John Galsworthy

John Galsworthy was born at Kingston Upon Thames in Surrey, England, on August 14th 1867 to a wealthy and well established family. His schooling was at Harrow and New College, Oxford before training as a barrister and being called to the bar in 1890. However, Law was not attractive to him and he travelled abroad becoming great friends with the novelist Joseph Conrad, then a first mate on a sailing ship.

In 1895 Galsworthy began an affair with Ada Nemesis Pearson Cooper, the wife of his cousin Major Arthur Galsworthy. The affair was kept a secret for 10 years till she at last divorced and they married on 23 September 1905.

John Galsworthy first published in 1897 with a collection of short stories entitled "The Four Winds". For the next 7 years he published these and all works under his pen name John Sinjohn. It was only upon the death of his father and the publication of "The Island Pharisees" in 1904 that he published as John Galsworthy. In this volume we have Villa Rubein ays and studies. They are the work of a supreme talent at the top of his game. Whilst today he is far more well know as a Nobel Prize winning novelist then he was considered a playwright dealing with social issues and the class system. He was appointed to the Order of Merit in 1929, after earlier turning down a knighthood, and awarded the Nobel Prize in 1932 though he was too ill to attend. John Galsworthy died from a brain tumour at his London home, Grove Lodge, Hampstead on January 31st 1933. In accordance with his will he was cremated at Woking with his ashes ther being scattered over the South Downs from an aeroplane.

He is now far better known for his novels, particularly The Forsyte Saga, his trilogy about the eponymous family of the same name. These books, as with many of his other works, deal with social class, upper-middle class lives in particular. Although always sympathetic to his characters, he reveals their insular, snobbish, and somewhat greedy attitudes and suffocating moral codes. He is now viewed as one of the first from the Edwardian era to challenge some of the ideals of society depicted in the literature of Victorian England.

In his writings he campaigns for a variety of causes, including prison reform, women's rights, animal welfare, and the opposition of censorship as well as a recurring theme of an unhappy marriage from the women's side. During World War I he worked in a hospital in France as an orderly after being passed over for military service.

He was appointed to the Order of Merit in 1929, after earlier turning down a knighthood, and awarded the Nobel Prize in 1932 though he was too ill to attend.

John Galsworthy died from a brain tumour at his London home, Grove Lodge, Hampstead on January 31st 1933. In accordance with his will he was cremated at Woking with his ashes then being scattered over the South Downs from an aeroplane.

Index of Contents

THE FIRST AND THE LAST

A DRAMA IN THREE SCENES

PERSONS OF THE PLAY
KEITH DARRANT, K.C.
LARRY DARRANT, His Brother.
WANDA.

THE SCENES

SCENE I. KEITH'S Study.

SCENE II. WANDA's Room.

SCENE III. The Same.

Between SCENE I. and SCENE II.—Thirty hours. Between SCENE II. and SCENE III.—Two months.

SCENE I

It is six o'clock of a November evening, in Keith Darrant's study. A large, dark-curtained room where the light from a single reading-lamp falling on Turkey carpet, on books beside a large armchair, on the deep blue-and-gold coffee service, makes a sort of oasis before a log fire. In red Turkish slippers and an old brown velvet coat, KEITH DARRANT sits asleep. He has a dark, clean-cut, clean-shaven face, dark grizzling hair, dark twisting eyebrows.

[The curtained door away out in the dim part of the room behind him is opened so softly that he does not wake. LARRY DARRANT enters and stands half lost in the curtain over the door. A thin figure, with a worn, high cheek-boned face, deep-sunk blue eyes and wavy hair all ruffled—a face which still has a certain beauty. He moves inwards along the wall, stands still again and utters a gasping sigh. KEITH stirs in his chair.]

KEITH
Who's there?

LARRY
[In a stifled voice] Only I—Larry.

KEITH [Half-waked]
Come in! I was asleep.

[He does not turn his head, staring sleepily at the fire.

[The sound of **LARRY's** breathing can be heard.

KEITH [Turning his head a little]
Well, Larry, what is it?

[**LARRY** comes skirting along the wall, as if craving its support, outside the radius of the light.

KEITH
[Staring] Are you ill?

LARRY stands still again and heaves a deep sigh.

KEITH [Rising, with his back to the fire, and staring at his brother]
What is it, man? [Then with a brutality born of nerves suddenly ruffled] Have you committed a murder that you stand there like a fish?

LARRY [In a whisper]
Yes, Keith.

KEITH [With vigorous disgust]

By Jove! Drunk again! [In a voice changed by sudden apprehension] What do you mean by coming here in this state? I told you—If you weren't my brother—! Come here, where I can we you! What's the matter with you, Larry?

[With a lurch **LARRY** leaves the shelter of the wall and sinks into a chair in the circle of light.

LARRY
It's true.

[**KEITH** steps quickly forward and stares down into his brother's eyes, where is a horrified wonder, as if they would never again get on terms with his face.

KEITH [Angry, bewildered-in a low voice]
What in God's name is this nonsense?

[He goes quickly over to the door and draws the curtain aside, to see that it is shut, then comes back to **LARRY,** who is huddling over the fire.

Come, Larry! Pull yourself together and drop exaggeration! What on earth do you mean?

LARRY [In a shrill outburst]
It's true, I tell you; I've killed a man.

KEITH [Bracing himself; coldly]
Be quiet!

[**LARRY** lifts his hands and wrings them.

KEITH [Utterly taken aback]
Why come here and tell me this?

LARRY
Whom should I tell, Keith? I came to ask what I'm to do—give myself up, or what?

KEITH
When—when—what—?

LARRY
Last night.

KEITH
Good God! How? Where? You'd better tell me quietly from the beginning. Here, drink this coffee; it'll clear your head.

[He pours out and hands him a cup of coffee. **LARRY** drinks it off.

LARRY
My head! Yes! It's like this, Keith—there's a girl—

KEITH
Women! Always women, with you! Well?

LARRY
A Polish girl. She—her father died over here when she was sixteen, and left her all alone. There was a mongrel living in the same house who married her—or pretended to. She's very pretty, Keith. He left her with a baby coming. She lost it, and nearly starved. Then another fellow took her on, and she lived with him two years, till that brute turned up again and made her go back to him. He used to beat her black and blue. He'd left her again when—I met her. She was taking anybody then.

[He stops, passes his hand over his lips, looks up at **KEITH**, and goes on defiantly.

I never met a sweeter woman, or a truer, that I swear. Woman! She's only twenty now! When I went to her last night, that devil had found her out again. He came for me—a bullying, great, hulking brute. Look!

[He touches a dark mark on his forehead.

I took his ugly throat, and when I let go—

[He stops and his hands drop.

KEITH
Yes?

LARRY [In a smothered voice]
Dead, Keith. I never knew till afterwards that she was hanging on to him—to h-help me.

[Again he wrings his hands.

KEITH [In a hard, dry voice]
What did you do then?

LARRY
We—we sat by it a long time.

KEITH
Well?

LARRY
Then I carried it on my back down the street, round a corner, to an archway.

KEITH
How far?

LARRY
About fifty yards.

KEITH
Was—did anyone see?

LARRY
No.

KEITH
What time?

LARRY
Three in the morning.

KEITH
And then?

LARRY
Went back to her.

KEITH
Why—in heaven's name?

LARRY
She way lonely and afraid. So was I, Keith.

KEITH
Where is this place?

LARRY
Forty-two Borrow Square, Soho.

KEITH
And the archway?

LARRY
Corner of Glove Lane.

KEITH
Good God! Why, I saw it in the paper this morning. They were talking of it in the Courts! [He snatches the evening paper from his armchair, and runs it over anal reads] Here it is again. "Body of a man was found this morning under an archway in Glove Lane. From marks about the throat grave suspicion of foul play are entertained. The body had apparently been robbed." My God! [Suddenly he turns] You saw this in the paper and dreamed it. D'you understand, Larry?—you dreamed it.

LARRY [Wistfully]
If only I had, Keith!

[**KEITH** makes a movement of his hands almost like his brother's.

KEITH
Did you take anything from the-body?

LARRY [Drawing an envelope from his pocket]
This dropped out while we were struggling.

KEITH [Snatching it and reading]
"Patrick Walenn"—Was that his name? "Simon's Hotel, Farrier Street, London." [Stooping, he puts it in the fire] No!—that makes me—[He bends to pluck it out, stays his hand, and stamps it suddenly further in with his foot] What in God's name made you come here and tell me? Don't you know I'm—I'm within an ace of a Judgeship?

LARRY [Simply]
Yes. You must know what I ought to do. I didn't, mean to kill him, Keith. I love the girl—I love her. What shall I do?

KEITH
Love!

LARRY [In a flash]
Love!—That swinish brute! A million creatures die every day, and not one of them deserves death as he did. But but I feel it here. [Touching his heart] Such an awful clutch, Keith. Help me if you can, old man. I may be no good, but I've never hurt a fly if I could help it.

[He buries his face in his hands.

KEITH
Steady, Larry! Let's think it out. You weren't seen, you say?

LARRY
It's a dark place, and dead night.

KEITH
When did you leave the girl again?

LARRY
About seven.

KEITH
Where did you go?

LARRY
To my rooms.

KEITH
To Fitzroy Street?

LARRY
Yes.

KEITH
What have you done since?

LARRY
Sat there—thinking.

KEITH
Not been out?

LARRY
No.

KEITH
Not seen the girl?

[**LARRY** shakes his head.

Will she give you away?

LARRY
Never.

KEITH
Or herself hysteria?

LARRY
No.

KEITH
Who knows of your relations with her?

LARRY
No one.

KEITH
No one?

LARRY
I don't know who should, Keith.

KEITH
Did anyone see you go in last night, when you first went to her?

LARRY
No. She lives on the ground floor. I've got keys.

KEITH
Give them to me.

[**LARRY** takes two keys from his pocket and hands them to his brother.

LARRY [Rising]
I can't be cut off from her!

KEITH
What! A girl like that?

LARRY [With a flash]
Yes, a girl like that.

KEITH [Moving his hand to put down old emotion]
What else have you that connects you with her?

LARRY
Nothing.

KEITH
In your rooms?

[**LARRY** shakes his head.

Photographs? Letters?

LARRY
No.

KEITH
Sure?

LARRY
Nothing.

KEITH
No one saw you going back to her?

[**LARRY** shakes his head.

KEITH
Nor leave in the morning? You can't be certain.

LARRY
I am.

KEITH
You were fortunate. Sit down again, man. I must think.

[He turns to the fire and leans his elbows on the mantelpiece and his head on his hands. **LARRY** Sits down again obediently.

KEITH
It's all too unlikely. It's monstrous!

LARRY [Sighing it out]
Yes.

KEITH
This Walenn—was it his first reappearance after an absence?

LARRY
Yes.

KEITH
How did he find out where she was?

LARRY
I don't know.

KEITH [Brutally]
How drunk were you?

LARRY
I was not drunk.

KEITH
How much had you drunk, then?

LARRY
A little claret—nothing!

KEITH
You say you didn't mean to kill him.

LARRY
God knows.

KEITH
That's something.

LARRY
He hit me.

[He holds up his hands.

I didn't know I was so strong.

KEITH
She was hanging on to him, you say?—That's ugly.

LARRY
She was scared for me.

KEITH
D'you mean she—loves you?

LARRY [Simply]
Yes, Keith.

KEITH [Brutally]
Can a woman like that love?

LARRY [Flashing out]
By God, you are a stony devil! Why not?

KEITH [Dryly]
I'm trying to get at truth. If you want me to help, I must know everything. What makes you think she's fond of you?

LARRY [With a crazy laugh]
Oh, you lawyer! Were you never in a woman's arms?

KEITH
I'm talking of love.

LARRY [Fiercely]
So am I. I tell you she's devoted. Did you ever pick up a lost dog? Well, she has the lost dog's love for me. And I for her; we picked each other up. I've never felt for another woman what I feel for her—she's been the saving of me!

KEITH [With a shrug]
What made you choose that archway?

LARRY
It was the first dark place.

KEITH
Did his face look as if he'd been strangled?

LARRY
Don't!

KEITH
Did it?

[**LARRY** bows his head.

KEITH
Very disfigured?

LARRY
Yes.

KEITH
Did you look to see if his clothes were marked?

LARRY
No.

KEITH
Why not?

LARRY [In an outburst]
I'm not made of iron, like you. Why not? If you had done it—!

KEITH [Holding up his hand]
You say he was disfigured. Would he be recognisable?

LARRY [Wearily]
 I don't know.

KEITH
When she lived with him last—where was that?

LARRY
In Pimlico, I think.

KEITH
Not Soho?

[**LARRY** shakes his head.

KEITH
How long has she been at this Soho place?

LARRY
Nearly a year.

KEITH

Living this life?

LARRY
Till she met me.

KEITH
Till, she met you? And you believe—?

LARRY [Starting up]
Keith!

KEITH [Again raising his hand]
Always in the same rooms?

LARRY [Subsiding]
Yes.

KEITH
What was he? A professional bully?

[**LARRY** nods.

KEITH
Spending most of his time abroad, I suppose.

LARRY
I think so.

KEITH
Can you say if he was known to the police?

LARRY
I've never heard.

[**KEITH** turns away and walks up and down; then, stopping at **LARRY's** chair, he speaks.

KEITH
Now listen, Larry. When you leave here, go straight home, and stay there till I give you leave to go out again. Promise.

LARRY
I promise.

KEITH
Is your promise worth anything?

LARRY [With one of his flashes]
"Unstable as water, he shall not excel!"

KEITH

Exactly. But if I'm to help you, you must do as I say. I must have time to think this out. Have you got money?

LARRY

Very little.

KEITH [Grimly]

Half-quarter day—yes, your quarter's always spent by then. If you're to get away—never mind, I can manage the money.

LARRY [Humbly]

You're very good, Keith; you've always been very good to me—I don't know why.

KEITH [Sardonically]

Privilege of A brother. As it happens, I'm thinking of myself and our family. You can't indulge yourself in killing without bringing ruin. My God! I suppose you realise that you've made me an accessory after the fact—me, King's counsel—sworn to the service of the Law, who, in a year or two, will have the trying of cases like yours! By heaven, Larry, you've surpassed yourself!

LARRY [Bringing out a little box]

I'd better have done with it.

KEITH

You fool! Give that to me.

LARRY [With a strange smite]

No.

[He holds up a tabloid between finger and thumb.

White magic, Keith! Just one—and they may do what they like to you, and you won't know it. Snap your fingers at all the tortures. It's a great comfort! Have one to keep by you?

KEITH

Come, Larry! Hand it over.

LARRY [Replacing the box]

Not quite! You've never killed a man, you see. [He gives that crazy laugh.] D'you remember that hammer when we were boys and you riled me, up in the long room? I had luck then. I had luck in Naples once. I nearly killed a driver for beating his poor brute of a horse. But now—! My God!

[He covers his face.

[**KEITH** touched, goes up and lays a hand on his shoulder.

KEITH

Come, Larry! Courage!

[**LARRY** looks up at him.

LARRY
All right, Keith; I'll try.

KEITH
Don't go out. Don't drink. Don't talk. Pull yourself together!

LARRY [Moving towards the door]
Don't keep me longer than you can help, Keith.

KEITH
No, no. Courage!

[**LARRY** reaches the door, turns as if to say something-finds no words, and goes.

KEITH [To the fire]
Courage! My God! I shall need it!

CURTAIN

SCENE II

At out eleven o'clock the following night an Wanda's room on the ground floor in Soho. In the light from one close-shaded electric bulb the room is but dimly visible. A dying fire burns on the left. A curtained window in the centre of the back wall. A door on the right. The furniture is plush-covered and commonplace, with a kind of shabby smartness. A couch, without back or arms, stands aslant, between window and fire.

[On this **WANDA** is sitting, her knees drawn up under her, staring at the embers. She has on only her nightgown and a wrapper over it; her bare feet are thrust into slippers. Her hands are crossed and pressed over her breast. She starts and looks up, listening. Her eyes are candid and startled, her face alabaster pale, and its pale brown hair, short and square-cut, curls towards her bare neck. The startled dark eyes and the faint rose of her lips are like colour-staining on a white mask.]

[Footsteps as of a policeman, very measured, pass on the pavement outside, and die away. She gets up and steals to the window, draws one curtain aside so that a chink of the night is seen. She opens the curtain wider, till the shape of a bare, witch-like tree becomes visible in the open space of the little Square on the far side of the road. The footsteps are heard once more coming nearer. **WANDA** closes the curtains and cranes back. They pass and die again. She moves away and looking down at the floor between door and couch, as though seeing something there; shudders; covers her eyes; goes back to the couch and down again just as before, to stare at the embers. Again she is startled by noise of the outer door being opened. She springs up, runs and turns the light by a switch close to the door. By the glimmer of the fire she can just be seen standing by the dark window-curtains, listening. There comes the sound of subdued knocking on her door. She stands in breathless terror. The knocking is repeated. The sound of a latchkey in the door is heard. Her terror leaves her. The door opens; a man enters in a dark, fur overcoat.

WANDA [In a voice of breathless relief, with a rather foreign accent]
Oh! it's you, Larry! Why did you knock? I was so frightened. Come in!

[She crosses quickly, and flings her arms round his neck.

[Recoiling—in a terror-stricken whisper.
Oh! Who is it?

KEITH [In a smothered voice]
A friend of Larry's. Don't be frightened.

[She has recoiled again to the window; and when he finds the switch and turns the light up, she is seen standing there holding her dark wrapper up to her throat, so that her face has an uncanny look of being detached from the body.

KEITH [Gently]
You needn't be afraid. I haven't come to do you harm—quite the contrary. [Holding up the keys] Larry wouldn't have given me these, would he, if he hadn't trusted me?

[**WANDA** does not move, staring like a spirit startled out of the flesh.

KEITH [After looking round him]
I'm sorry to have startled you.

WANDA [In a whisper]
Who are you, please?

KEITH
Larry's brother.

[**WANDA**, with a sigh of utter relief, steals forward to the couch and sinks down. **KEITH** goes up to her.

KEITH
He'd told me.

WANDA [Clasping her hands round her knees.]
Yes?

KEITH
An awful business!

WANDA
Yes; oh, yes! Awful—it is awful!

KEITH [Staring round him again.]
In this room?

WANDA
Just where you are standing. I see him now, always falling.

KEITH [Moved by the gentle despair in her voice]
You—look very young. What's your name?

WANDA
Wanda.

KEITH
Are you fond of Larry?

WANDA
I would die for him!

[A moment's silence.

KEITH
I—I've come to see what you can do to save him.

WANDA [Wistfully]
You would not deceive me. You are really his brother?

KEITH
I swear it.

WANDA [Clasping her hands]
If I can save him! Won't you sit down?

KEITH [Drawing up a chair and sitting]
This, man, your—your husband, before he came here the night before last—how long since you saw him?

WANDA
Eighteen month.

KEITH
Does anyone about here know you are his wife?

WANDA
No. I came here to live a bad life. Nobody know me. I am quite alone.

KEITH
They've discovered who he was—you know that?

WANDA

No; I have not dared to go out.

KEITH

Well, they have; and they'll look for anyone connected with him, of course.

WANDA

He never let people think I was married to him. I don't know if I was—really. We went to an office and signed our names; but he was a wicked man. He treated many, I think, like me.

KEITH

Did my brother ever see him before?

WANDA

Never! And that man first went for him.

KEITH

Yes. I saw the mark. Have you a servant?

WANDA

No. A woman come at nine in the morning for an hour.

KEITH

Does she know Larry?

WANDA

No. He is always gone.

KEITH

Friends—acquaintances?

WANDA

No; I am verree quiet. Since I know your brother, I see no one, sare.

KEITH [Sharply]

Do you mean that?

WANDA

Oh, yes! I love him. Nobody come here but him for a long time now.

KEITH

How long?

WANDA

Five month.

KEITH

So you have not been out since—?

[WANDA shakes her head.

What have you been doing?

WANDA [Simply]
Crying.

[Pressing her hands to her breast.

He is in danger because of me. I am so afraid for him.

KEITH [Checking her emotion]
Look at me.

[She looks at him.

If the worst comes, and this man is traced to you, can you trust yourself not to give Larry away?

WANDA
[Rising and pointing to the fire] Look! I have burned all the things he have given me—even his picture. Now I have nothing from him.

KEITH [Who has risen too]
Good! One more question. Do the police know you—because—of your life?

[She looks at him intently, and shakes her, head.

You know where Larry lives?

WANDA
Yes.

KEITH
You mustn't go there, and he mustn't come to you.

[She bows her head; then, suddenly comes close to him.

WANDA
Please do not take him from me altogether. I will be so careful. I will not do anything to hurt him. But if I cannot see him sometimes, I shall die. Please do not take him from me.

[She catches his hand and presses it desperately between her own.

KEITH
Leave that to me. I'm going to do all I can.

WANDA [Looking up into his face]

But you will be kind?

[Suddenly she bends and kisses his hand. **KEITH** draws his hand away, and she recoils a little humbly, looking up at him again. Suddenly she stands rigid, listening.

WANDA [In a whisper]
Listen! Someone—out there!

She darts past him and turns out the light. There is a knock on the door. They are now close together between door and window.

WANDA [Whispering]
Oh! Who is it?

KEITH [Under his breath]
You said no one comes but Larry.

WANDA
Yes, and you have his keys. Oh! if it is Larry! I must open!

[**KEITH** shrinks back against the wall. **WANDA** goes to the door.

WANDA [Opening the door an inch]
Yes? Please? Who?

[A thin streak of light from a bull's-eye lantern outside plays over the wall. A Policeman's voice says: "All right, Miss. Your outer door's open. You ought to keep it shut after dark, you know."

WANDA
Thank you, air.

[The sound of retreating footsteps, of the outer door closing. **WANDA** shuts the door.

A policeman!

KEITH [Moving from the wall]
Curse! I must have left that door. [Suddenly-turning up the light] You told me they didn't know you.

WANDA [Sighing]
I did not think they did, sir. It is so long I was not out in the town; not since I had Larry.

[**KEITH** gives her an intent look, then crosses to the fire. He stands there a moment, looking down, then turns to the girl, who has crept back to the couch.

KEITH [Half to himself]
After your life, who can believe—? Look here! You drifted together and you'll drift apart, you know. Better for him to get away and make a clean cut of it.

WANDA [Uttering a little moaning sound]

Oh, sir! May I not love, because I have been bad? I was only sixteen when that man spoiled me. If you knew—

KEITH

I'm thinking of Larry. With you, his danger is much greater. There's a good chance as things are going. You may wreck it. And for what? Just a few months more of—well—you know.

WANDA [Standing at the head of the couch and touching her eyes with her hands]

Oh, sir! Look! It is true. He is my life. Don't take him away from me.

KEITH [Moved and restless]

You must know what Larry is. He'll never stick to you.

WANDA [Simply]

He will, sir.

KEITH [Energetically]

The last man on earth to stick to anything! But for the sake of a whim he'll risk his life and the honour of all his family. I know him.

WANDA

No, no, you do not. It is I who know him.

KEITH

Now, now! At any moment they may find out your connection with that man. So long as Larry goes on with you, he's tied to this murder, don't you see?

WANDA [Coming close to him]

But he love me. Oh, sir! he love me!

KEITH

Larry has loved dozens of women.

WANDA

Yes, but—[Her face quivers].

KEITH [Brusquely]

Don't cry! If I give you money, will you disappear, for his sake?

WANDA [With a moan]

It will be in the water, then. There will be no cruel men there.

KEITH

Ah! First Larry, then you! Come now. It's better for you both. A few months, and you'll forget you ever met.

WANDA [Looking wildly up]
I will go if Larry say I must. But not to live. No! [Simply] I could not, sir.

[**KEITH**, moved, is silent.

WANDA
I could not live without Larry. What is left for a girl like me—when she once love? It is finish.

KEITH
I don't want you to go back to that life.

WANDA
No; you do not care what I do. Why should you? I tell you I will go if Larry say I must.

KEITH
That's not enough. You know that. You must take it out of his hands. He will never give up his present for the sake of his future. If you're as fond of him as you say, you'll help to save him.

WANDA [Below her breath]
Yes! Oh, yes! But do not keep him long from me—I beg!

[She sinks to the floor and clasps his knees.

KEITH
Well, well! Get up.

[There is a tap on the window-pane.

Listen!

[A faint, peculiar whistle.

WANDA [Springing up]
Larry! Oh, thank God!

[She runs to the door, opens it, and goes out to bring him in. **KEITH** stands waiting, facing the open doorway.

[**LARRY** entering with **WANDA** just behind him.

LARRY
Keith!

KEITH [Grimly]
So much for your promise not to go out!

LARRY
I've been waiting in for you all day. I couldn't stand it any longer.

KEITH
Exactly!

LARRY
Well, what's the sentence, brother? Transportation for life and then to be fined forty pounds'?

KEITH
So you can joke, can you?

LARRY
Must.

KEITH
A boat leaves for the Argentine the day after to-morrow; you must go by it.

LARRY [Putting his arms round **WANDA**, who is standing motionless with her eyes fixed on him]
Together, Keith?

KEITH
You can't go together. I'll send her by the next boat.

LARRY
Swear?

KEITH
Yes. You're lucky they're on a false scent.

LARRY
What?

KEITH
You haven't seen it?

LARRY
I've seen nothing, not even a paper.

KEITH
They've taken up a vagabond who robbed the body. He pawned a snake-shaped ring, and they identified this Walenn by it. I've been down and seen him charged myself.

LARRY
With murder?

WANDA [Faintly]
Larry!

KEITH

He's in no danger. They always get the wrong man first. It'll do him no harm to be locked up a bit—hyena like that. Better in prison, anyway, than sleeping out under archways in this weather.

LARRY
What was he like, Keith?

KEITH
A little yellow, ragged, lame, unshaven scarecrow of a chap. They were fools to think he could have had the strength.

LARRY
What! [In an awed voice] Why, I saw him—after I left you last night.

KEITH
You? Where?

LARRY
By the archway.

KEITH
You went back there?

LARRY
It draws you, Keith.

KEITH
You're mad, I think.

LARRY
I talked to him, and he said, "Thank you for this little chat. It's worth more than money when you're down." Little grey man like a shaggy animal. And a newspaper boy came up and said: "That's right, guv'nors! 'Ere's where they found the body—very spot. They 'yn't got 'im yet."

[He laughs; and the terrified girl presses herself against him.

LARRY
An innocent man!

KEITH
He's in no danger, I tell you. He could never have strangled—Why, he hadn't the strength of a kitten. Now, Larry! I'll take your berth to-morrow. Here's money

[He brings out a pile of notes and puts them on the couch.

You can make a new life of it out there together presently, in the sun.

LARRY [In a whisper]

In the sun! "A cup of wine and thou." [Suddenly] How can I, Keith? I must see how it goes with that poor devil.

KEITH
Bosh! Dismiss it from your mind; there's not nearly enough evidence.

LARRY
Not?

KEITH
No. You've got your chance. Take it like a man.

LARRY [With a strange smile—to the girl]
Shall we, Wanda?

WANDA
Oh, Larry!

LARRY [Picking the notes up from the couch]
Take them back, Keith.

KEITH
What! I tell you no jury would convict; and if they did, no judge would hang. A ghoul who can rob a dead body, ought to be in prison. He did worse than you.

LARRY
It won't do, Keith. I must see it out.

KEITH
Don't be a fool!

LARRY
I've still got some kind of honour. If I clear out before I know, I shall have none—nor peace. Take them, Keith, or I'll put them in the fire.

KEITH [Taking back the notes; bitterly]
I suppose I may ask you not to be entirely oblivious of our name. Or is that unworthy of your honour?

LARRY [Hanging his head]
I'm awfully sorry, Keith; awfully sorry, old man.

KEITH [sternly]
You owe it to me—to our name—to our dead mother—to do nothing anyway till we see what happens.

LARRY
I know. I'll do nothing without you, Keith.

KEITH [Taking up his hat]

Can I trust you?

[He stares hard at his brother.

LARRY
You can trust me.

KEITH
Swear?

LARRY
I swear.

KEITH
Remember, nothing! Good night!

LARRY
Good night!

[**KEITH** goes. **LARRY** Sits down on the couch sand stares at the fire. The **GIRL** steals up and slips her arms about him.

LARRY
An innocent man!

WANDA
Oh, Larry! But so are you. What did we want—to kill that man? Never! Oh! kiss me!

[**LARRY** turns his face. She kisses his lips.

I have suffered so—not seein' you. Don't leave me again—don't! Stay here. Isn't it good to be together?—Oh! Poor Larry! How tired you look!—Stay with me. I am so frightened all alone. So frightened they will take you from me.

LARRY
Poor child!

WANDA
No, no! Don't look like that!

LARRY
You're shivering.

WANDA
I will make up the fire. Love me, Larry! I want to forget.

LARRY

The poorest little wretch on God's earth—locked up—for me! A little wild animal, locked up. There he goes, up and down, up and down—in his cage—don't you see him?—looking for a place to gnaw his way through—little grey rat.

[He gets up and roams about.

WANDA
No, no! I can't bear it! Don't frighten me more!

[He comes back and takes her in his arms.

LARRY
There, there! [He kisses her closed eyes.]

WANDA [Without moving]
If we could sleep a little—wouldn't it be nice?

LARRY
Sleep?

WANDA [Raising herself]
Promise to stay with me—to stay here for good, Larry. I will cook for you; I will make you so comfortable. They will find him innocent. And then—Oh, Larry! in the sun-right away—far from this horrible country. How lovely!

[Trying to get him to look at her.

Larry!

LARRY [With a movement to free 'himself]
To the edge of the world-and—over!

WANDA
No, no! No, no! You don't want me to die, Larry, do you? I shall if you leave me. Let us be happy! Love me!

LARRY [With a laugh]
Ah! Let's be happy and shut out the sight of him. Who cares? Millions suffer for no mortal reason. Let's be strong, like Keith. No! I won't leave you, Wanda. Let's forget everything except ourselves. [Suddenly] There he goes-up and down!

WANDA [Moaning]
No, no! See! I will pray to the Virgin. She will pity us!

[She falls on her knees and clasps her hands, praying. Her lips move. **LARRY** stands motionless, with arms crossed, and on his face are yearning and mockery, love and despair.

LARRY [Whispering]

Pray for us! Bravo! Pray away!

[Suddenly the **GIRL** stretches out her arms and lifts her face with a look of ecstasy.

What?

WANDA
She is smiling! We shall be happy soon.

LARRY [Bending down over her]
Poor child! When we die, Wanda, let's go together. We should keep each other warm out in the dark.

WANDA [Raising her hands to his face]
Yes! oh, yes! If you die I could not—I could not go on living!

CURTAIN

SCENE III

TWO MONTHS LATER

Wanda's room. Daylight is just beginning to fail of a January afternoon. The table is laid for supper, with decanters of wine.

WANDA is standing at the window looking out at the wintry trees of the Square beyond the pavement. A newspaper Boy's voice is heard coming nearer.

VOICE
Pyper! Glove Lyne murder! Trial and verdict! [Receding] Verdict! Pyper!

[**WANDA** throws up the window as if to call to him, checks herself, closes it and runs to the door. She opens it, but recoils into the room. **KEITH** is standing there. He comes in.

KEITH
Where's Larry?

WANDA
He went to the trial. I could not keep him from it. The trial—Oh! what has happened, sir?

KEITH [Savagely]
Guilty! Sentence of death! Fools!—idiots!

WANDA
Of death!

[For a moment she seems about to swoon.

KEITH
Girl! girl! It may all depend on you. Larry's still living here?

WANDA
Yes.

KEITH
I must wait for him.

WANDA
Will you sit down, please?

KEITH [Shaking his head]
Are you ready to go away at any time?

WANDA
Yes, yes; always I am ready.

KEITH
And he?

WANDA
Yes—but now! What will he do? That poor man!

KEITH
A graveyard thief—a ghoul!

WANDA
Perhaps he was hungry. I have been hungry: you do things then that you would not. Larry has thought of him in prison so much all these weeks. Oh! what shall we do now?

KEITH
Listen! Help me. Don't let Larry out of your sight. I must see how things go. They'll never hang this wretch. [He grips her arms] Now, we must stop Larry from giving himself up. He's fool enough. D'you understand?

WANDA
Yes. But why has he not come in? Oh! If he have, already!

KEITH [Letting go her arms]
My God! If the police come—find me here—[He moves to the door] No, he wouldn't without seeing you first. He's sure to come. Watch him like a lynx. Don't let him go without you.

WANDA [Clasping her hands on her breast]
I will try, sir.

KEITH

Listen!

[A key is heard in the lock.

It's he!

[**LARRY** enters. He is holding a great bunch of pink lilies and white narcissus. His face tells nothing. **KEITH** looks from him to the girl, who stands motionless.

LARRY
Keith! So you've seen?

KEITH
The thing can't stand. I'll stop it somehow. But you must give me time, Larry.

LARRY [Calmly]
Still looking after your honour, Keith!

KEITH [Grimly]
Think my reasons what you like.

WANDA [Softly]
Larry!

[**LARRY** puts his arm round her.

LARRY
Sorry, old man.

KEITH
This man can and shall get off. I want your solemn promise that you won't give yourself up, nor even go out till I've seen you again.

LARRY
I give it.

KEITH [Looking from one to the other]
By the memory of our mother, swear that.

LARRY [With a smile]
I swear.

KEITH
I have your oath—both of you—both of you. I'm going at once to see what can be done.

LARRY [Softly]
Good luck, brother.

[**KEITH** goes out.

WANDA [Putting her hands on **LARRY's** breast]
What does it mean?

LARRY
Supper, child—I've had nothing all day. Put these lilies in water.

[She takes the lilies and obediently puts them into a vase. **LARRY** pours wine into a deep-coloured glass and drinks it off.]

We've had a good time, Wanda. Best time I ever had, these last two months; and nothing but the bill to pay.

WANDA [Clasping him desperately]
Oh, Larry! Larry!

LARRY [Holding her away to look at her.]
Take off those things and put on a bridal garment.

WANDA
Promise me—wherever you go, I go too. Promise! Larry, you think I haven't seen, all these weeks. But I have seen everything; all in your heart, always. You cannot hide from me. I knew—I knew! Oh, if we might go away into the sun! Oh! Larry—couldn't we? [She searches his eyes with hers—then shuddering] Well! If it must be dark—I don't care, if I may go in your arms. In prison we could not be together. I am ready. Only love me first. Don't let me cry before I go. Oh! Larry, will there be much pain?

LARRY [In a choked voice]
No pain, my pretty.

WANDA [With a little sigh]
It is a pity.

LARRY
If you had seen him, as I have, all day, being tortured. Wanda,—we shall be out of it. [The wine mounting to his head] We shall be free in the dark; free of their cursed inhumanities. I hate this world—I loathe it! I hate its God-forsaken savagery; its pride and smugness! Keith's world—all righteous will-power and success. We're no good here, you and I—we were cast out at birth—soft, will-less—better dead. No fear, Keith! I'm staying indoors.

[He pours wine into two glasses.

Drink it up!

[Obediently **WANDA** drinks, and he also.

Now go and make yourself beautiful.

WANDA [Seizing him in her arms]
Oh, Larry!

LARRY [Touching her face and hair]
Hanged by the neck until he's dead—for what I did.

[**WANDA** takes a long look at his face, slips her arms from him, and goes out through the curtains below the fireplace.

[**LARRY** feels in his pocket, brings out the little box, opens it, fingers the white tabloids.

LARRY
Two each—after food. [He laughs and puts back the box] Oh! my girl!

[The sound of a piano playing a faint festive tune is heard afar off. He mutters, staring at the fire.

[Flames-flame, and flicker-ashes.

LARRY
"No more, no more, the moon is dead, And all the people in it."

[He sits on the couch with a piece of paper on his knees, adding a few words with a stylo pen to what is already written.]

[The **GIRL**, in a silk wrapper, coming back through the curtains, watches him.

LARRY [Looking up]
It's all here—I've confessed. [Reading]
"Please bury us together." "LAURENCE DARRANT. "January 28th, about six p.m."

They'll find us in the morning. Come and have supper, my dear love.

[The **GIRL** creeps forward. He rises, puts his arm round her, and with her arm twined round him, smiling into each other's faces, they go to the table and sit down.

[The curtain falls for a few seconds to indicate the passage of three hours. When it rises again, the lovers are lying on the couch, in each other's arms, the lilies stream about them. The girl's bare arm is round **LARRY'S** neck. Her eyes are closed; his are open and sightless. There is no light but fire-light.

[A knocking on the door and the sound of a key turned in the lock. **KEITH** enters. He stands a moment bewildered by the half-light, then calls sharply: "Larry!" and turns up the light. Seeing the forms on the couch, he recoils a moment. Then, glancing at the table and empty decanters, goes up to the couch.

KEITH [Muttering]
Asleep! Drunk! Ugh!

[Suddenly he bends, touches LARRY, and springs back.]

KEITH
What!

[He bends again, shakes him and calls.

KEITH
Larry! Larry!

[Then, motionless, he stares down at his brother's open, sightless eyes. Suddenly he wets his finger and holds it to the **GIRL'S** lips, then to **LARRY'S**.

[He bends and listens at their hearts; catches sight of the little box lying between them and takes it up.

My God!

[Then, raising himself, he closes his brother's eyes, and as he does so, catches sight of a paper pinned to the couch; detaches it and reads:]

"I, Lawrence Darrant, about to die by my own hand confess that I—"

[He reads on silently, in horror; finishes, letting the paper drop, and recoils from the couch on to a chair at the dishevelled supper table. Aghast, he sits there. Suddenly he mutters:]

If I leave that there—my name—my whole future!

[He springs up, takes up the paper again, and again reads.]

My God! It's ruin!

[He makes as if to tear it across, stops, and looks down at those two; covers his eyes with his hand; drops the paper and rushes to the door. But he stops there and comes back, magnetised, as it were, by that paper. He takes it up once more and thrusts it into his pocket.

[The footsteps of a **POLICEMAN** pass, slow and regular, outside. His face crisps and quivers; he stands listening till they die away. Then he snatches the paper from his pocket, and goes past the foot of the couch to the fore.

All my—No! Let him hang!

[He thrusts the paper into the fire, stamps it down with his foot, watches it writhe and blacken. Then suddenly clutching his head, he turns to the bodies on the couch. Panting and like a man demented, he recoils past the head of the couch, and rushing to the window, draws the curtains and throws the window up for air. Out in the darkness rises the witch-like skeleton tree, where a dark shape seems hanging. **KEITH** starts back.]

What's that? What—!

[He shuts the window and draws the dark curtains across it again.

Fool! Nothing!

[Clenching his fists, he draws himself up, steadying himself with all his might. Then slowly he moves to the door, stands a second like a carved figure, his face hard as stone.

[Deliberately he turns out the light, opens the door, and goes.

[The still bodies lie there before the fire which is licking at the last blackened wafer.

CURTAIN

THE LITTLE MAN

A FARCICAL MORALITY IN THREE SCENES

CHARACTERS
THE LITTLE MAN.
THE AMERICAN.
THE ENGLISHMAN
THE ENGLISHWOMAN.
THE GERMAN
THE DUTCH BOY.
THE MOTHER.
THE BABY.
THE WAITER.
THE STATION OFFICIAL.
THE POLICEMAN.
THE PORTER.

SCENE I

Afternoon, on the departure platform of an Austrian railway station. At several little tables outside the buffet persons are taking refreshment, served by a pale young waiter. On a seat against the wall of the buffet a woman of lowly station is sitting beside two large bundles, on one of which she has placed her baby, swathed in a black shawl.

WAITER [Approaching a table whereat sit an English traveller and his wife]
Two coffee?

ENGLISHMAN [Paying]
Thanks. [To his wife, in an Oxford voice] Sugar?

ENGLISHWOMAN [In a Cambridge voice]
One.

AMERICAN TRAVELLER [With field-glasses and a pocket camera from another table]
Waiter, I'd like to have you get my eggs. I've been sitting here quite a while.

WAITER
Yes, sare.

GERMAN TRAVELLER
'Kellner, bezahlen'! [His voice is, like his moustache, stiff and brushed up at the ends. His figure also is stiff and his hair a little grey; clearly once, if not now, a colonel.]

WAITER
'Komm' gleich'!

[The **BABY** on the bundle wails. The **MOTHER** takes it up to soothe it. A young, red-cheeked **DUTCHMAN** at the fourth table stops eating and laughs.]

AMERICAN
My eggs! Get a wiggle on you!

WAITER
Yes, sare. [He rapidly recedes.]

[A **LITTLE MAN** in a soft hat is seen to the right of tables. He stands a moment looking after the hurrying waiter, then seats himself at the fifth table.

ENGLISHMAN [Looking at his watch]
Ten minutes more.

ENGLISHWOMAN
Bother!

AMERICAN [Addressing them]
'Pears as if they'd a prejudice against eggs here, anyway.

[The **ENGLISH** look at him, but do not speak.

GERMAN
[In creditable English] In these places man can get nothing.

[The **WAITER** comes flying back with a compote for the **DUTCH YOUTH**, who pays.

GERMAN

'Kellner, bezahlen'!

WAITER
'Eine Krone sechzig'.

[The **GERMAN** pays.

AMERICAN [Rising, and taking out his watch—blandly]
See here. If I don't get my eggs before this watch ticks twenty, there'll be another waiter in heaven.

WAITER [Flying]
'Komm' gleich'!

AMERICAN [Seeking sympathy]
I'm gettin' kind of mad!

[The **ENGLISHMAN** halves his newspaper and hands the advertisement half to his wife. The **BABY** wails. The **MOTHER** rocks it.

[The **DUTCH YOUTH** stops eating and laughs. The **GERMAN** lights a cigarette. The **LITTLE MAN** sits motionless, nursing his hat. The **WAITER** comes flying back with the eggs and places them before the **AMERICAN**.

AMERICAN [Putting away his watch]
Good! I don't like trouble. How much?

[He pays and eats. The **WAITER** stands a moment at the edge of the platform and passes his hand across his brow. The **LITTLE MAN** eyes him and speaks gently.

LITTLE MAN
Herr Ober!

[The **WAITER** turns.

Might I have a glass of beer?

WAITER
Yes, sare.

LITTLE MAN
Thank you very much.

[The **WAITER** goes.

AMERICAN
[Pausing in the deglutition of his eggs—affably] Pardon me, sir; I'd like to have you tell me why you called that little bit of a feller "Herr Ober." Reckon you would know what that means? Mr. Head Waiter.

LITTLE MAN
Yes, yes.

AMERICAN
I smile.

LITTLE MAN
Oughtn't I to call him that?

GERMAN [Abruptly]
'Nein—Kellner'.

AMERICAN
Why, yes! Just "waiter."

[The **ENGLISHWOMAN** looks round her paper for a second. The **DUTCH YOUTH** stops eating and laughs. The **LITTLE MAN** gazes from face to face and nurses his hat.

LITTLE MAN
I didn't want to hurt his feelings.

GERMAN
Gott!

AMERICAN
In my country we're very democratic—but that's quite a proposition.

ENGLISHMAN [Handling coffee-pot, to his wife]
More?

ENGLISHWOMAN
No, thanks.

GERMAN [Abruptly]
These fellows—if you treat them in this manner, at once they take liberties. You see, you will not get your beer.

[As he speaks the **WAITER** returns, bringing the **LITTLE MAN'S** beer, then retires.

AMERICAN
That 'pears to be one up to democracy. [To the **LITTLE MAN**] I judge you go in for brotherhood?

LITTLE MAN [Startled]
Oh, no!

AMERICAN

I take considerable stock in Leo Tolstoi myself. Grand man—grand-souled apparatus. But I guess you've got to pinch those waiters some to make 'em skip. [To the **ENGLISH**, who have carelessly looked his way for a moment] You'll appreciate that, the way he acted about my eggs.

[The **ENGLISH** make faint motions with their chins and avert their eyes.

[To the **WAITER**, who is standing at the door of the buffet

AMERICAN
Waiter! Flash of beer—jump, now!

WAITER
'Komm' gleich'!

GERMAN
'Cigarren'!

WAITER
'Schon'!

[He disappears.

AMERICAN [Affably—to the **LITTLE MAN**]
Now, if I don't get that flash of beer quicker'n you got yours, I shall admire.

GERMAN [Abruptly]
Tolstoi is nothing 'nichts'! No good! Ha?

AMERICAN [Relishing the approach of argument]
Well, that is a matter of temperament. Now, I'm all for equality. See that poor woman there—very humble woman—there she sits among us with her baby. Perhaps you'd like to locate her somewhere else?

GERMAN [Shrugging].
Tolstoi is 'sentimentalisch'. Nietzsche is the true philosopher, the only one.

AMERICAN
Well, that's quite in the prospectus—very stimulating party—old Nietch—virgin mind. But give me Leo! [He turns to the red-cheeked **YOUTH**] What do you opine, sir? I guess by your labels you'll be Dutch. Do they read Tolstoi in your country?

[The **DUTCH YOUTH** laughs.

AMERICAN
That is a very luminous answer.

GERMAN
Tolstoi is nothing. Man should himself express. He must push—he must be strong.

AMERICAN
That is so. In America we believe in virility; we like a man to expand. But we believe in brotherhood too. We draw the line at niggers; but we aspire. Social barriers and distinctions we've not much use for.

ENGLISHMAN
Do you feel a draught?

ENGLISHWOMAN [With a shiver of her shoulder toward the **AMERICAN**]
I do—rather.

GERMAN
Wait! You are a young people.

AMERICAN
That is so; there are no flies on us. [To the **LITTLE MAN**, who has been gazing eagerly from face to face] Say! I'd like to have you give us your sentiments in relation to the duty of man.

[The **LITTLE MAN**, fidgets, and is about to opens his mouth.

AMERICAN
For example—is it your opinion that we should kill off the weak and diseased, and all that can't jump around?

GERMAN [Nodding]
'Ja, ja'! That is coming.

LITTLE MAN [Looking from face to face]
They might be me.

[The **DUTCH YOUTH** laughs.

AMERICAN
[Reproving him with a look] That's true humility. 'Tisn't grammar. Now, here's a proposition that brings it nearer the bone: Would you step out of your way to help them when it was liable to bring you trouble?

GERMAN
'Nein, nein'! That is stupid.

LITTLE MAN [Eager but wistful]
I'm afraid not. Of course one wants to—There was St Francis d'Assisi and St Julien L'Hospitalier, and—

AMERICAN
Very lofty dispositions. Guess they died of them. [He rises] Shake hands, sir—my name is—[He hands a card] I am an ice-machine maker. [He shakes the **LITTLE MAN's** hand] I like your sentiments—I feel kind of brotherly.

[Catching sight of the **WAITER** appearing in the doorway.

Waiter; where to h-ll is that glass of beer?

GERMAN
Cigarren!

WAITER
'Komm' gleich'!

ENGLISHMAN [Consulting watch]
Train's late.

ENGLISHWOMAN
Really! Nuisance!

[A station **POLICEMAN**, very square and uniformed, passes and repasses.

AMERICAN [Resuming his seat—to the **GERMAN**]
Now, we don't have so much of that in America. Guess we feel more to trust in human nature.

GERMAN
Ah! ha! you will bresently find there is nothing in him but self.

LITTLE MAN [Wistfully]
Don't you believe in human nature?

AMERICAN
Very stimulating question.

[He looks round for opinions. The **DUTCH YOUTH** laughs.

ENGLISHMAN [Holding out his half of the paper to his wife]
Swap!

[His wife swaps.

GERMAN
In human nature I believe so far as I can see him—no more.

AMERICAN
Now that 'pears to me kind o' blasphemy. I believe in heroism. I opine there's not one of us settin' around here that's not a hero—give him the occasion.

LITTLE MAN
Oh! Do you believe that?

AMERICAN

Well! I judge a hero is just a person that'll help another at the expense of himself. Take that poor woman there. Well, now, she's a heroine, I guess. She would die for her baby any old time.

GERMAN
Animals will die for their babies. That is nothing.

AMERICAN
I carry it further. I postulate we would all die for that baby if a locomotive was to trundle up right here and try to handle it. [To the **GERMAN**] I guess you don't know how good you are.

[As the **GERMAN** is twisting up the ends of his moustache—to the **ENGLISHWOMAN**]

I should like to have you express an opinion, ma'am.

ENGLISHWOMAN
I beg your pardon.

AMERICAN
The English are very humanitarian; they have a very high sense of duty. So have the Germans, so have the Americans. [To the **DUTCH YOUTH**] I judge even in your little country they have that. This is an epoch of equality and high-toned ideals. [To the **LITTLE MAN**] What is your nationality, sir?

LITTLE MAN
I'm afraid I'm nothing particular. My father was half-English and half-American, and my mother half-German and half-Dutch.

AMERICAN
My! That's a bit streaky, any old way. [The **POLICEMAN** passes again] Now, I don't believe we've much use any more for those gentlemen in buttons. We've grown kind of mild—we don't think of self as we used to do.

[The **WAITER** has appeared in the doorway.

GERMAN
[In a voice of thunder] 'Cigarren! Donnerwetter'!

AMERICAN [Shaking his fist at the vanishing **WAITER**]
That flash of beer!

WAITER
'Komm' gleich'!

AMERICAN
A little more, and he will join George Washington! I was about to remark when he intruded: In this year of grace 1913 the kingdom of Christ is quite a going concern. We are mighty near universal brotherhood. The colonel here [He indicates the **GERMAN**] is a man of blood and iron, but give him an opportunity to be magnanimous, and he'll be right there. Oh, sir! yep!

[The **GERMAN**, with a profound mixture of pleasure and cynicism, brushes up the ends of his moustache.

LITTLE MAN
I wonder. One wants to, but somehow—

[He shakes his head.

AMERICAN
You seem kind of skeery about that. You've had experience, maybe. I'm an optimist—I think we're bound to make the devil hum in the near future. I opine we shall occasion a good deal of trouble to that old party. There's about to be a holocaust of selfish interests. The colonel there with old-man Nietch he won't know himself. There's going to be a very sacred opportunity.

[As he speaks, the voice of a **RAILWAY OFFICIAL** is heard an the distance calling out in German. It approaches, and the words become audible.

GERMAN [Startled]
'Der Teufel'! [He gets up, and seizes the bag beside him.]

[The **STATION OFFICIAL** has appeared; he stands for a moment casting his commands at the seated group. The **DUTCH YOUTH** also rises, and takes his coat and hat. The **OFFICIAL** turns on his heel and retires still issuing directions.]

ENGLISHMAN
What does he say?

GERMAN
Our drain has come in, de oder platform; only one minute we haf.

[All, have risen in a fluster.

AMERICAN
Now, that's very provoking. I won't get that flash of beer.

[There is a general scurry to gather coats and hats and wraps, during which the lowly **WOMAN** is seen making desperate attempts to deal with her baby and the two large bundles. Quite defeated, she suddenly puts all down, wrings her hands, and cries out: "Herr Jesu! Hilfe!" The flying procession turn their heads at that strange cry.]

AMERICAN
What's that? Help?

[He continues to run. The **LITTLE MAN** spins round, rushes back, picks up baby and bundle on which it was seated.

LITTLE MAN
Come along, good woman, come along!

[The **WOMAN** picks up the other bundle and they run.

[The **WAITER**, appearing in the doorway with the bottle of beer, watches with his tired smile.

CURTAIN

SCENE II

A second-class compartment of a corridor carriage, in motion. In it are seated the **ENGLISHMAN** and his **WIFE**, opposite each other at the corridor end, she with her face to the engine, he with his back. Both are somewhat protected from the rest of the travellers by newspapers. Next to her sits the **GERMAN**, and opposite him sits the **AMERICAN**; next the **AMERICAN** in one window corner is seated the **DUTCH YOUTH**; the other window corner is taken by the **GERMAN'S** bag. The silence is only broken by the slight rushing noise of the train's progression and the crackling of the English newspapers.

AMERICAN [Turning to the **DUTCH YOUTH**]
Guess I'd like that window raised; it's kind of chilly after that old run they gave us.

[The **DUTCH YOUTH** laughs, and goes through the motions of raising the window. The **ENGLISH** regard the operation with uneasy irritation. The **GERMAN** opens his bag, which reposes on the corner seat next him, and takes out a book.

AMERICAN
The Germans are great readers. Very stimulating practice. I read most anything myself!

[The **GERMAN** holds up the book so that the title may be read.

AMERICAN
"Don Quixote"—fine book. We Americans take considerable stock in old man Quixote. Bit of a wildcat—but we don't laugh at him.

GERMAN
He is dead. Dead as a sheep. A good thing, too.

AMERICAN
In America we have still quite an amount of chivalry.

GERMAN
Chivalry is nothing 'sentimentalisch'. In modern days—no good. A man must push, he must pull.

AMERICAN
So you say. But I judge your form of chivalry is sacrifice to the state. We allow more freedom to the individual soul. Where there's something little and weak, we feel it kind of noble to give up to it. That way we feel elevated.

[As he speaks there is seen in the corridor doorway the **LITTLE MAN**, with the **WOMAN'S BABY** still on his arm and the bundle held in the other hand. He peers in anxiously. The **ENGLISH**, acutely conscious, try to dissociate themselves from his presence with their papers. The **DUTCH YOUTH** laughs.

GERMAN
'Ach'! So!

AMERICAN
Dear me!

LITTLE MAN
Is there room? I can't find a seat.

AMERICAN
Why, yes! There's a seat for one.

LITTLE MAN [Depositing bundle outside, and heaving **BABY**]
May I?

AMERICAN
Come right in!

[The **GERMAN** sulkily moves his bag. The **LITTLE MAN** comes in and seats himself gingerly.

AMERICAN
Where's the mother?

LITTLE MAN [Ruefully]
Afraid she got left behind.

[The **DUTCH YOUTH** laughs. The **ENGLISH** unconsciously emerge from their newspapers.

AMERICAN
My! That would appear to be quite a domestic incident.

[The **ENGLISHMAN** suddenly utters a profound "Ha, Ha!" and disappears behind his paper. And that paper and the one opposite are seen to shake, and little sguirls and squeaks emerge.

GERMAN
And you haf got her bundle, and her baby. Ha!

[He cackles drily.

AMERICAN [Gravely]
I smile. I guess Providence has played it pretty low down on you. It's sure acted real mean.

[The **BABY** wails, and the **LITTLE MAN** jigs it with a sort of gentle desperation, looking apologetically from face to face. His wistful glance renews the fore of merriment wherever it alights. The **AMERICAN** alone preserves a gravity which seems incapable of being broken.

AMERICAN
Maybe you'd better get off right smart and restore that baby. There's nothing can act madder than a mother.

LITTLE MAN
Poor thing, yes! What she must be suffering!

[A gale of laughter shakes the carriage. The **ENGLISH** for a moment drop their papers, the better to indulge. The **LITTLE MAN** smiles a wintry smile.

AMERICAN [In a lull]
How did it eventuate?

LITTLE MAN
We got there just as the train was going to start; and I jumped, thinking I could help her up. But it moved too quickly, and—and left her.

[The gale of laughter blows up again.

AMERICAN
Guess I'd have thrown the baby out to her.

LITTLE MAN
I was afraid the poor little thing might break.

[The **BABY** wails; the **LITTLE MAN** heaves it; the gale of laughter blows.

AMERICAN [Gravely]
It's highly entertaining—not for the baby. What kind of an old baby is it, anyway? [He sniff's] I judge it's a bit—niffy.

LITTLE MAN
Afraid I've hardly looked at it yet.

AMERICAN
Which end up is it?

LITTLE MAN
Oh! I think the right end. Yes, yes, it is.

AMERICAN
Well, that's something. Maybe you should hold it out of window a bit. Very excitable things, babies!

ENGLISHWOMAN [Galvanized]

No, no!

ENGLISHMAN [Touching her knee]
My dear!

AMERICAN
You are right, ma'am. I opine there's a draught out there. This baby is precious. We've all of us got stock in this baby in a manner of speaking. This is a little bit of universal brotherhood. Is it a woman baby?

LITTLE MAN
I—I can only see the top of its head.

AMERICAN
You can't always tell from that. It looks kind of over-wrapped up. Maybe it had better be unbound.

GERMAN
'Nein, nein, nein'!

AMERICAN
I think you are very likely right, colonel. It might be a pity to unbind that baby. I guess the lady should be consulted in this matter.

ENGLISHWOMAN
Yes, yes, of course—!

ENGLISHMAN [Touching her]
Let it be! Little beggar seems all right.

AMERICAN
That would seem only known to Providence at this moment. I judge it might be due to humanity to look at its face.

LITTLE MAN [Gladly]
It's sucking my' finger. There, there—nice little thing—there!

AMERICAN
I would surmise in your leisure moments you have created babies, sir?

LITTLE MAN
Oh! no—indeed, no.

AMERICAN
Dear me!—That is a loss. [Addressing himself to the carriage at large] I think we may esteem ourselves fortunate to have this little stranger right here with us. Demonstrates what a hold the little and weak have upon us nowadays. The colonel here—a man of blood and iron—there he sits quite calm next door to it. [He sniffs] Now, this baby is rather chastening—that is a sign of grace, in the colonel—that is true heroism.

LITTLE MAN [Faintly]

I—I can see its face a little now.

[All bend forward.]

AMERICAN

What sort of a physiognomy has it, anyway?

LITTLE MAN [Still faintly]

I don't see anything but—but spots.

GERMAN

 Oh! Ha! Pfui!

[The **DUTCH YOUTH** laughs.

AMERICAN

I am told that is not uncommon amongst babies. Perhaps we could have you inform us, ma'am.

ENGLISHWOMAN

Yes, of course—only what sort of—

LITTLE MAN

They seem all over its—[At the slight recoil of everyone] I feel sure it's—it's quite a good baby underneath.

AMERICAN

That will be rather difficult to come at. I'm just a bit sensitive. I've very little use for affections of the epidermis.

GERMAN

 Pfui!

[He has edged away as far as he can get, and is lighting a big cigar.

[The **DUTCH YOUTH** draws his legs back.

AMERICAN [Also taking out a cigar]

I guess it would be well to fumigate this carriage. Does it suffer, do you think?

LITTLE MAN [Peering]

Really, I don't—I'm not sure—I know so little about babies. I think it would have a nice expression—if—if it showed.

AMERICAN

Is it kind of boiled looking?

LITTLE MAN
Yes—yes, it is.

AMERICAN [Looking gravely round]
I judge this baby has the measles.

[The **GERMAN** screws himself spasmodically against the arm of the **ENGLISHWOMAN'S** seat.]

ENGLISHWOMAN
Poor little thing! Shall I—?

[She half rises.

ENGLISHMAN [Touching her]
No, no—Dash it!

AMERICAN
I honour your emotion, ma'am. It does credit to us all. But I sympathize with your husband too. The measles is a very important pestilence in connection with a grown woman.

LITTLE MAN
It likes my finger awfully. Really, it's rather a sweet baby.

AMERICAN
[Sniffing] Well, that would appear to be quite a question. About them spots, now? Are they rosy?

LITTLE MAN
No-o; they're dark, almost black.

GERMAN
Gott! Typhus! [He bounds up on to the arm of the **ENGLISHWOMAN'S** Seat.

AMERICAN
Typhus! That's quite an indisposition!

[The **DUTCH YOUTH** rises suddenly, and bolts out into the corridor. He is followed by the **GERMAN**, puffing clouds of smoke. The **ENGLISH** and **AMERICAN** sit a moment longer without speaking. The **ENGLISHWOMAN'S** face is turned with a curious expression—half pity, half fear—towards the **LITTLE MAN.** Then the **ENGLISHMAN** gets up.

ENGLISHMAN
Bit stuffy for you here, dear, isn't it?

[He puts his arm through hers, raises her, and almost pushes her through the doorway. She goes, still looking back.]

AMERICAN [Gravely]
There's nothing I admire more'n courage. Guess I'll go and smoke in the corridor.

[As he goes out the **LITTLE MAN** looks very wistfully after him. Screwing up his mouth and nose, he holds the **BABY** away from him and wavers; then rising, he puts it on the seat opposite and goes through the motions of letting down the window. Having done so he looks at the **BABY**, who has begun to wail. Suddenly he raises his hands and clasps them, like a child praying. Since, however, the **BABY** does not stop wailing, he hovers over it in indecision; then, picking it up, sits down again to dandle it, with his face turned toward the open window. Finding that it still wails, he begins to sing to it in a cracked little voice. It is charmed at once. While he is singing, the **AMERICAN** appears in the corridor. Letting down the passage window, he stands there in the doorway with the draught blowing his hair and the smoke of his cigar all about him. The **LITTLE MAN** stops singing and shifts the shawl higher to protect the **BABY'S** head from the draught.

AMERICAN [Gravely]
This is the most sublime spectacle I have ever envisaged. There ought to be a record of this.

[The **LITTLE MAN** looks at him, wondering. You are typical, sir, of the sentiments of modern Christianity. You illustrate the deepest feelings in the heart of every man.

[The **LITTLE MAN** rises with the **BABY** and a movement of approach.]

Guess I'm wanted in the dining-car.

[He vanishes. The **LITTLE MAN** sits down again, but back to the engine, away from the draught, and looks out of the window, patiently jogging the **BABY** On his knee.]

CURTAIN

SCENE III

An arrival platform. The **LITTLE MAN**, with the **BABY** and the bundle, is standing disconsolate, while travellers pass and luggage is being carried by. A **STATION OFFICIAL**, accompanied by a **POLICEMAN**, appears from a doorway, behind him.

OFFICIAL [Consulting telegram in his hand]
'Das ist der Herr'.

[They advance to the **LITTLE MAN**.

OFFICIAL
'Sie haben einen Buben gestohlen'?

LITTLE MAN
I only speak English and American.

OFFICIAL
'Dies ist nicht Ihr Bube'?

[He touches the **BABY**.

LITTLE MAN
[Shaking his head] Take care—it's ill.

[The **MAN** does not understand.

Ill—the baby—

OFFICIAL [Shaking his head]
'Verstehe nicht'. Dis is nod your baby? No?

LITTLE MAN [Shaking his head violently]
No, it is not. No.

OFFICIAL [Tapping the telegram]
Gut! You are 'rested.

[He signs to the **POLICEMAN**, who takes the **LITTLE MAN's** arm.

LITTLE MAN
Why? I don't want the poor baby.

OFFICIAL [Lifting the bundle]
'Dies ist nicht Ihr Gepack'—pag?

LITTLE MAN
No.

OFFICIAL
Gut! You are 'rested.

LITTLE MAN
I only took it for the poor woman. I'm not a thief—I'm—I'm—

OFFICIAL [Shaking head] Verstehe nicht.

[The **LITTLE MAN** tries to tear his hair. The disturbed **BABY** wails.

LITTLE MAN
[Dandling it as best he can] There, there—poor, poor!

OFFICIAL
Halt still! You are 'rested. It is all right.

LITTLE MAN
Where is the mother?

OFFICIAL
She comet by next drain. Das telegram say: 'Halt einen Herren mit schwarzem Buben and schwarzem Gepäck'. 'Rest gentleman mit black baby and black—pag.

[The **LITTLE MAN** turns up his eyes to heaven.]

OFFICIAL
'Komm mit us'.

[They take the **LITTLE MAN** toward the door from which they have come. A voice stops them.]

AMERICAN [Speaking from as far away as may be]
Just a moment!

[The **OFFICIAL** stops; the **LITTLE MAN** also stops and sits down on a bench against the wall. The **POLICEMAN** stands stolidly beside him. The **AMERICAN** approaches a step or two, beckoning; the **OFFICIAL** goes up to him.

AMERICAN
Guess you've got an angel from heaven there! What's the gentleman in buttons for?

OFFICIAL
'Was ist das'?

AMERICAN
Is there anybody here that can understand American?

OFFICIAL
'Verstehe nicht'.

AMERICAN
Well, just watch my gestures. I was saying—

[He points to the **LITTLE MAN**, then makes gestures of flying]

—you have an angel from heaven there. You have there a man in whom Gawd [He points upward] takes quite an amount of stock. You have no call to arrest him.

[He makes the gesture of arrest.

No, Sir. Providence has acted pretty mean, loading off that baby on him.

[He makes the motion of dandling.

The little man has a heart of gold.

[He points to his heart, and takes out a gold coin.

OFFICIAL [Thinking he is about to be bribed]
'Aber, das ist zu viel'!

AMERICAN
Now, don't rattle me! [Pointing to the **LITTLE MAN**] Man [Pointing to his heart] 'Herz' [Pointing to the coin] 'von' Gold. This is a flower of the field—he don't want no gentleman in buttons to pluck him up.

[A little crowd is gathering, including the Two **ENGLISH**, the **GERMAN**, and the **DUTCH YOUTH**.

OFFICIAL
'Verstehe absolut nichts'. [He taps the telegram] 'Ich muss mein' duty do.

AMERICAN
But I'm telling you. This is a white man. This is probably the whitest man on Gawd's earth.

OFFICIAL
'Das macht nichts'—gut or no gut, I muss mein duty do.

[He turns to go toward the **LITTLE MAN**.

AMERICAN
Oh! Very well, arrest him; do your duty. This baby has typhus.

[At the word "typhus" the **OFFICIAL** stops.

AMERICAN [Making gestures]
First-class typhus, black typhus, schwarzen typhus. Now you have it. I'm kind o' sorry for you and the gentleman in buttons. Do your duty!

OFFICIAL
Typhus? Der Bub—die baby hat typhus?

AMERICAN
I'm telling you.

OFFICIAL
Gott im Himmel!

AMERICAN [Spotting the **GERMAN** in the little throng]
Here's a gentleman will corroborate me.

OFFICIAL [Much disturbed, and signing to the **POLICEMAN** to stand clear]
Typhus! 'Aber das ist grasslich'!

AMERICAN
I kind o' thought you'd feel like that.

OFFICIAL
'Die Sanitatsmachine! Gleich'!

[A **PORTER** goes to get it. From either side the broken half-moon of persons stand gazing at the **LITTLE MAN**, who sits unhappily dandling the **BABY** in the centre.

OFFICIAL [Raising his hands]
'Was zu thun'?

AMERICAN
Guess you'd better isolate the baby.

[A silence, during which the **LITTLE MAN** is heard faintly whistling and clucking to the **BABY**.

OFFICIAL [Referring once more to his telegram]
"'Rest gentleman mit black baby." [Shaking his head] Wir must de gentleman hold. [To the **GERMAN**]
'Bitte, mein Herr, sagen Sie ihm, den Buben zu niedersetzen'.

[He makes the gesture of deposit.

GERMAN [To the **LITTLE MAN**]
He say: Put down the baby.

[The **LITTLE MAN** shakes his head, and continues to dandle the **BABY**.

OFFICIAL
You must.

[The **LITTLE MAN** glowers, in silence.

ENGLISHMAN [In background—muttering]
Good man!

GERMAN
His spirit ever denies.

OFFICIAL [Again making his gesture]
'Aber er muss'!

[The **LITTLE MAN** makes a face at him.]

'Sag' Ihm': Instantly put down baby, and komm' mit us.

[The **BABY** wails.]

LITTLE MAN
Leave the poor ill baby here alone? Be—be—be d—d to you!

AMERICAN [Jumping on to a trunk—with enthusiasm]
  Bully!

[The **ENGLISH** clap their hands; the **DUTCH YOUTH** laughs. The **OFFICIAL** is muttering, greatly incensed.]

AMERICAN
What does that body-snatcher say?

GERMAN
 He say this man use the baby to save himself from arrest. Very smart he say.

AMERICAN
I judge you do him an injustice.

[Showing off the **LITTLE MAN** with a sweep of his arm.

This is a white man. He's got a black baby, and he won' leave it in the lurch. Guess we would all act noble that way, give us the chance.

[The **LITTLE MAN** rises, holding out the **BABY**, and advances a step or two. The half-moon at once gives, increasing its size; the **AMERICAN** climbs on to a higher trunk. The **LITTLE MAN** retires and again sits down.

AMERICAN [Addressing the **OFFICIAL**]
Guess you'd better go out of business and wait for the mother.

OFFICIAL [Stamping his foot]
Die Mutter sall 'rested be for taking out baby mit typhus. Ha! [To the **LITTLE MAN**] Put ze baby down!

[The **LITTLE MAN** smiles.]

Do you 'ear?

AMERICAN [Addressing the **OFFICIAL**]
Now, see here. 'Pears to me you don't suspicion just how beautiful this is. Here we have a man giving his life for that old baby that's got no claim on him. This is not a baby of his own making. No, sir, this is a very Christ-like proposition in the gentleman.

OFFICIAL
Put ze baby down, or ich will goummand someone it to do.

AMERICAN
That will be very interesting to watch.

OFFICIAL [To **POLICEMAN**]
Dake it vrom him.

[The **POLICEMAN** mutters, but does not.

AMERICAN [To the **GERMAN**]
Guess I lost that.

GERMAN
He say he is not his officier.

AMERICAN
That just tickles me to death.

OFFICIAL [Looking round]
Vill nobody dake ze Bub'?

ENGLISHWOMAN [Moving a step faintly]
Yes—I—

ENGLISHMAN [Grasping her arm]
By Jove! Will you!

OFFICIAL [Gathering himself for a great effort to take the **BABY**, and advancing two steps]
Zen I goummand you—

[He stops and his voice dies away.

Zit dere!

AMERICAN
My! That's wonderful. What a man this is! What a sublime sense of duty!

[The **DUTCH YOUTH** laughs. The **OFFICIAL** turns on him, but as he does so the **MOTHER** of the **BABY** is seen hurrying.

MOTHER
'Ach! Ach! Mei' Bubi'!

[Her face is illumined; she is about to rush to the **LITTLE MAN**.

OFFICIAL [To the **POLICEMAN**]
'Nimm die Frau'!

[The **POLICEMAN** catches hold of the **WOMAN**.

OFFICIAL [To the frightened **WOMAN**]
'Warum haben Sie einen Buben mit Typhus mit ausgebracht'?

AMERICAN [Eagerly, from his perch]
What was that? I don't want to miss any.

GERMAN
He say: Why did you a baby with typhus with you bring out?

AMERICAN
Well, that's quite a question.

[He takes out the field-glasses slung around him and adjusts them on the **BABY**.]

MOTHER [Bewildered]
Mei' Bubi—Typhus—aber Typhus? [She shakes her head violently] 'Nein, nein, nein! Typhus'!

OFFICIAL
Er hat Typhus.

MOTHER [Shaking her head]
'Nein, nein, nein'!

AMERICAN [Looking through his glasses]
Guess she's kind of right! I judge the typhus is where the baby' slobbered on the shawl, and it's come off on him.

[The **DUTCH YOUTH** laughs.

OFFICIAL [Turning on him furiously]
Er hat Typhus.

AMERICAN
Now, that's where you slop over. Come right here.

[The **OFFICIAL** mounts, and looks through the glasses.

AMERICAN [To the **LITTLE MAN**]
Skin out the baby's leg. If we don't locate spots on that, it'll be good enough for me.

[The **LITTLE MAN** fumbles Out the **BABY'S** little white foot.

MOTHER
Mei' Bubi!

[She tries to break away.

AMERICAN
White as a banana. [To the **OFFICIAL**—affably] Guess you've made kind of a fool of us with your old typhus.

OFFICIAL
Lass die Frau!

[The **POLICEMAN** lets her go, and she rushes to her **BABY**.]

MOTHER
Mei' Bubi!

[The **BABY**, exchanging the warmth of the **LITTLE MAN** for the momentary chill of its **MOTHER**, wails.

OFFICIAL [Descending and beckoning to the **POLICEMAN**]
'Sie wollen den Herrn accusiren'?

[The **POLICEMAN** takes the **LITTLE MAN's** arm.]

AMERICAN
What's that? They goin' to pitch him after all?

[The **MOTHER**, still hugging her **BABY**, who has stopped crying, gazes at the **LITTLE MAN**, who sits dazedly looking up. Suddenly she drops on her knees, and with her free hand lifts his booted foot and kisses it.

AMERICAN [Waving his hat]
Ra! Ra!

[He descends swiftly, goes up to the **LITTLE MAN**, whose arm the **POLICEMAN** has dropped, and takes his hand]

Brother; I am proud to know you. This is one of the greatest moments I have ever experienced.

[Displaying the **LITTLE MAN** to the assembled company.

I think I sense the situation when I say that we all esteem it an honour to breathe the rather inferior atmosphere of this station here Along with our little friend. I guess we shall all go home and treasure the memory of his face as the whitest thing in our museum of recollections. And perhaps this good woman will also go home and wash the face of our little brother here. I am inspired with a new faith in mankind. Ladies and gentlemen, I wish to present to you a sure-enough saint—only wants a halo, to be transfigured. [To the **LITTLE MAN**] Stand right up.

[The **LITTLE MAN** stands up bewildered. They come about him. The **OFFICIAL** bows to him, the **POLICEMAN** salutes him. The **DUTCH YOUTH** shakes his head and laughs. The **GERMAN** draws himself up very straight, and bows quickly twice. The **ENGLISHMAN** and his WIFE approach at least two steps, then, thinking better of it, turn to each other and recede. The **MOTHER** kisses his hand. The **PORTER** returning with the Sanitatsmachine, turns it on from behind, and its pinkish shower, goldened by a ray of sunlight, falls around the **LITTLE MAN's** head, transfiguring it as he stands with eyes upraised to see whence the portent comes.

AMERICAN [Rushing forward and dropping on his knees]
Hold on just a minute! Guess I'll take a snapshot of the miracle.

[He adjusts his pocket camera.

This ought to look bully!

CURTAIN

HALL-MARKED

A SATIRIC TRIFLE

CHARACTERS
HERSELF.
LADY ELLA.
THE SQUIRE.
THE MAID.
MAUD.
THE RECTOR.
THE DOCTOR.
THE CABMAN.
HANNIBAL and EDWARD

HALL-MARKED

The scene is the sitting-room and verandah of **HER** bungalow.

The room is pleasant, and along the back, where the verandah runs, it seems all window, both French and casement. There is a door right and a door left. The day is bright; the time morning.

[**HERSELF**, dripping wet, comes running along the verandah, through the French window, with a wet Scotch terrier in her arms. She vanishes through the door left. A little pause, and **LADY ELLA** comes running, dry, thin, refined, and agitated. She halts where the tracks of water cease at the door left. A little pause, and **MAUD** comes running, fairly dry, stolid, breathless, and dragging a bull-dog, wet, breathless, and stout, by the crutch end of her 'en-tout-cas'.

LADY ELLA
Don't bring Hannibal in till I know where she's put Edward!

MAUD [Brutally, to **HANNIBAL**]
Bad dog! Bad dog!

[**HANNIBAL** snuffles.

LADY ELLA

Maud, do take him out! Tie him up. Here! [She takes out a lace handkerchief] No—something stronger! Poor darling Edward! [To **HANNIBAL**] You are a bad dog!

[**HANNIBAL** snuffles.

MAUD
Edward began it, Ella. [To **HANNIBAL**] Bad dog! Bad dog!

[**HANNIBAL** snuffles.

LADY ELLA
Tie him up outside. Here, take my scarf. Where is my poor treasure? [She removes her scarf] Catch! His ear's torn; I saw it.

MAUD [Taking the scarf, to **HANNIBAL**]
Now!

[**HANNIBAL** snuffles.

[She ties the scarf to his collar.

He smells horrible. Bad dog—getting into ponds to fight!

LADY ELLA
Tie him up, Maud. I must try in here.

[Their husbands, **THE SQUIRE** and **THE RECTOR**, come hastening along the verandah.

MAUD [To **THE RECTOR**] Smell him, Bertie! [To **THE SQUIRE**] You might have that pond drained, Squire!

[She takes **HANNIBAL** out, and ties him to the verandah. **THE SQUIRE** and **RECTOR** Come in. **LADY ELLA** is knocking on the door left.

HER VOICE
All right! I've bound him up!

LADY ELLA
May I come in?

HER VOICE
Just a second! I've got nothing on.

[**LADY ELLA** recoils. **THE SQUIRE** and **RECTOR** make an involuntary movement of approach.

LADY ELLA
Oh! There you are!

THE RECTOR [Doubtfully]

I was just going to wade in—

LADY ELLA
Hannibal would have killed him, if she hadn't rushed in!

THE SQUIRE
Done him good, little beast!

LADY ELLA
Why didn't you go in, Tommy?

THE SQUIRE
Well, I would—only she—

LADY ELLA
I can't think how she got Edward out of Hannibal's awful mouth!

MAUD [Without—to **HANNIBAL**, who is snuffling on the verandah and straining at the scarf]
Bad dog!

LADY ELLA
We must simply thank her tremendously! I shall never forget the way she ran in, with her skirts up to her waist!

THE SQUIRE
By Jove! No. It was topping.

LADY ELLA
Her clothes must be ruined. That pond—ugh! [She wrinkles her nose] Tommy, do have it drained.

THE RECTOR [Dreamily]
I don't remember her face in church.

THE SQUIRE
Ah! Yes. Who is she? Pretty woman!

LADY ELLA
I must get the Vet. to Edward. [To **THE SQUIRE**] Tommy, do exert yourself!

[**MAUD** re-enters.

THE SQUIRE
All right! [Exerting himself] Here's a bell!

HER VOICE [Through the door]
The bleeding's stopped. Shall I send him in to you?

LADY ELLA

Oh, please! Poor darling!

[They listen.

[**LADY ELLA**, prepares to receive **EDWARD**. **THE SQUIRE** and **RECTOR** stand transfixed. The door opens, and a bare arm gently pushes **EDWARD** forth. He is bandaged with a smooth towel. There is a snuffle— **HANNIBAL** has broken the scarf, outside.

LADY ELLA [Aghast]
Look! Hannibal's loose! Maud—Tommy. [To **THE RECTOR**] You!

[The **THREE** rush to prevent **HANNIBAL** from re-entering.]

LADY ELLA [To **EDWARD**]
Yes, I know—you'd like to! You SHALL bite him when it's safe. Oh! my darling, you DO—[She sniffs].

[**MAUD** and **THE SQUIRE** re-enter.]

Have you tied him properly this time?

MAUD
With Bertie's braces.

LADY ELLA
Oh! but—

MAUD
It's all right; they're almost leather.

[**THE RECTOR** re-enters, with a slight look of insecurity.

LADY ELLA
Rector, are you sure it's safe?

THE RECTOR [Hitching at his trousers]
No, indeed, LADY Ella—I—

LADY ELLA
Tommy, do lend a hand!

THE SQUIRE
All right, Ella; all right! He doesn't mean what you mean!

LADY ELLA [Transferring **EDWARD** to **THE SQUIRE**]
Hold him, Tommy. He's sure to smell out Hannibal!

THE SQUIRE [Taking **EDWARD** by the collar, and holding his own nose]

Jove! Clever if he can smell anything but himself. Phew! She ought to have the Victoria Cross for goin' in that pond.

[The door opens, and **HERSELF** appears; a fine, frank, handsome woman, in a man's orange-coloured motor-coat, hastily thrown on over the substrata of costume.

SHE
So very sorry—had to have a bath, and change, of course!

LADY ELLA
We're so awfully grateful to you. It was splendid.

MAUD
Quite.

THE RECTOR
[Rather holding himself together] Heroic! I was just myself about to—

THE SQUIRE [Restraining **EDWARD**]
Little beast will fight—must apologise—you were too quick for me—

[He looks up at her. She is smiling, and regarding the wounded dog, her head benevolently on one side.

SHE
Poor dears! They thought they were so safe in that nice pond!

LADY ELLA
Is he very badly torn?

SHE
Rather nasty. There ought to be a stitch or two put in his ear.

LADY ELLA
I thought so. Tommy, do—

THE SQUIRE
All right. Am I to let him go?

LADY ELLA
No.

MAUD
The fly's outside. Bertie, run and tell Jarvis to drive in for the Vet.

THE RECTOR [Gentle and embarrassed]
Run? Well, Maud—I—

SHE

The doctor would sew it up. My maid can go round.

[HANNIBAL. appears at the open casement with the broken braces dangling from his collar.

LADY ELLA
Look! Catch him! Rector!

MAUD
Bertie! Catch him!

[THE RECTOR seizes HANNIBAL, but is seen to be in difficulties with his garments. HERSELF, who has gone out left, returns, with a leather strop in one hand and a pair of braces in the other.

SHE
Take this strop—he can't break that. And would these be any good to you?

[SHE hands the braces to MAUD and goes out on to the verandah and hastily away. MAUD, transferring the braces to THE RECTOR, goes out, draws HANNIBAL from the casement window, and secures him with the strap. THE RECTOR sits suddenly with the braces in his hands. There is a moment's peace.

LADY ELLA
Splendid, isn't she? I do admire her.

THE SQUIRE
She's all there.

THE RECTOR [Feelingly]
Most kind.

[He looks ruefully at the braces and at LADY ELLA. A silence. MAUD reappears at the door and stands gazing at the braces.

THE SQUIRE [Suddenly]
Eh?

MAUD
Yes.

THE SQUIRE [Looking at his wife]
Ah!

LADY ELLA [Absorbed in EDWARD]
Poor darling!

THE SQUIRE [Bluntly]
Ella, the Rector wants to get up!

THE RECTOR [Gently]

Perhaps—just for a moment—

LADY ELLA
Oh!

[She turns to the wall.

[**THE RECTOR**, screened by his **WIFE**, retires on to the verandah to adjust his garments.]

THE SQUIRE [Meditating]
So she's married!

LADY ELLA [Absorbed in **EDWARD**]
Why?

THE SQUIRE
Braces.

LADY ELLA
Oh! Yes. We ought to ask them to dinner, Tommy.

THE SQUIRE
Ah! Yes. Wonder who they are?

[**THE RECTOR** and **MAUD** reappear.

THE RECTOR
Really very good of her to lend her husband's—I was—er—quite—

MAUD
That'll do, Bertie.

[**THEY** see **HER** returning along the verandah, followed by a sandy, red-faced gentleman in leather leggings, with a needle and cotton in his hand.

HERSELF
Caught the doctor just starting, So lucky!

LADY ELLA
Oh! Thank goodness!

DOCTOR
How do, Lady Ella? How do, Squire?—how do, Rector? [To **MAUD**] How de do? This the beastie? I see. Quite! Who'll hold him for me?

LADY ELLA
Oh! I!

HERSELF
D'you know, I think I'd better. It's so dreadful when it's your own, isn't it? Shall we go in here, doctor? Come along, pretty boy!

[She takes **EDWARD**, and they pass into the room, left.

LADY ELLA
I dreaded it. She is splendid!

THE SQUIRE
Dogs take to her. That's a sure sign.

THE RECTOR
Little things—one can always tell.

THE SQUIRE
Something very attractive about her—what! Fine build of woman.

MAUD
I shall get hold of her for parish work.

THE RECTOR
Ah! Excellent—excellent! Do!

THE SQUIRE
Wonder if her husband shoots? She seems quite-er—quite—

LADY ELLA [Watching the door]
Quite! Altogether charming; one of the nicest faces I ever saw.

[**THE DOCTOR** comes out alone.

Oh! Doctor—have you? is it—?

DOCTOR
Right as rain! She held him like an angel—he just licked her, and never made a sound.

LADY ELLA
Poor darling! Can I—

[She signs toward the door.

DOCTOR
Better leave 'em a minute. She's moppin' 'im off. [He wrinkles his nose] Wonderful clever hands!

THE SQUIRE
I say—who is she?

DOCTOR [Looking from face to face with a dubious and rather quizzical expression]
Who? Well—there you have me! All I know is she's a first-rate nurse—been helpin' me with a case in Ditch Lane. Nice woman, too—thorough good sort! Quite an acquisition here. H'm! [Again that quizzical glance] Excuse me hurryin' off—very late. Good-bye, Rector. Good-bye, Lady Ella. Good-bye!

[He goes. A silence.

THE SQUIRE
H'm! I suppose we ought to be a bit careful.

[JARVIS, flyman of the old school, has appeared on the verandah.

JARVIS [To **THE RECTOR**] Beg pardon, sir. Is the little dog all right?

MAUD
Yes.

JARVIS [Touching his hat]
Seein' you've missed your train, m'm, shall I wait, and take you 'ome again?

MAUD
No.

JARVIS
Cert'nly, m'm. [He touches his hat with a circular gesture, and is about to withdraw.]

LADY ELLA
Oh, Jarvis—what's the name of the people here?

JARVIS
Challenger's the name I've driven 'em in, my lady.

THE SQUIRE
Challenger? Sounds like a hound. What's he like?

JARVIS [Scratching his head]
Wears a soft 'at, sir.

THE SQUIRE
H'm! Ah!

JARVIS
Very nice gentleman, very nice lady. 'Elped me with my old mare when she 'ad the 'ighsteria last week—couldn't 'a' been kinder if they'd 'a' been angels from 'eaven. Wonderful fond o' dumb animals, the two of 'em. I don't pay no attention to gossip, meself.

MAUD
Gossip? What gossip?

JARVIS [Backing]
Did I make use of the word, m'm? You'll excuse me, I'm sure. There's always talk where there's newcomers. I takes people as I finds 'em.

THE RECTOR
Yes, yes, Jarvis—quite—quite right!

JARVIS
Yes, sir. I've—I've got a 'abit that way at my time o' life.

MAUD [Sharply]
How long have they been here, Jarvis?

JARVIS
Well—er—a matter of three weeks, m'm.

[A slight involuntary stir.

JARVIS [Apologetic]
Of course, in my profession I can't afford to take notice of whether there's the trifle of a ring between 'em, as the sayin' is. 'Tisn't 'ardly my business like.

[A silence.

LADY ELLA
[Suddenly] Er—thank you, Jarvis; you needn't wait.

JARVIS
No, m'lady. Your service, sir—service, m'm.

[He goes. A silence.

THE SQUIRE [Drawing a little closer]
Three weeks? I say—er—wasn't there a book?

THE RECTOR [Abstracted]
Three weeks—I certainly haven't seen them in church.

MAUD
A trifle of a ring!

LADY ELLA [Impulsively]
Oh, bother! I'm sure she's all right. And if she isn't, I don't care. She's been much too splendid.

THE SQUIRE
Must think of the village. Didn't quite like the doctor's way of puttin' us off.

LADY ELLA
The poor darling owes his life to her.

THE SQUIRE
H'm! Dash it! Yes! Can't forget the way she ran into that stinkin' pond.

MAUD
Had she a wedding-ring on?

[They look at each other, but no one knows.

LADY ELLA
Well, I'm not going to be ungrateful.

THE SQUIRE
It'd be dashed awkward—mustn't take a false step, Ella.

THE RECTOR
And I've got his braces!

[He puts his hand to his waist.

MAUD [Warningly]
Bertie!

THE SQUIRE
That's all right, Rector—we're goin' to be perfectly polite, and—and—thank her, and all that.

LADY ELLA
We can see she's a good sort. What does it matter?

MAUD
My dear Ella! "What does it matter!" We've got to know.

THE RECTOR
We do want light.

THE SQUIRE
I'll ring the bell. [He rings.]

[They look at each other aghast.

LADY ELLA
What did you ring for, Tommy?

THE SQUIRE [Flabbergasted]
God knows!

MAUD
Somebody'll come.

THE SQUIRE
Rector—you—you've got to—

MAUD
Yes, Bertie.

THE RECTOR
Dear me! But—er—what—er—How?

THE SQUIRE [Deeply-to himself]
The whole thing's damn delicate.

[The door right is opened and a **MAID** appears. She is a determined-looking female. They face her in silence.]

THE RECTOR
Er—er—your master is not in?

THE MAID
No. 'E's gone up to London.

THE RECTOR
Er—Mr Challenger, I think?

THE MAID
Yes.

THE RECTOR
Yes! Er—quite so

THE MAID [Eyeing them]
D'you want—Mrs Challenger?

THE RECTOR
Ah! Not precisely—

THE SQUIRE [To him in a low, determined voice]
Go on.

THE RECTOR [Desperately]
I asked because there was a—a—Mr. Challenger I used to know in the 'nineties, and I thought—you wouldn't happen to know how long they've been married? My friend marr—

THE MAID
Three weeks.

THE RECTOR
Quite so—quite so! I shall hope it will turn out to be—Er—thank you—Ha!

LADY ELLA
Our dog has been fighting with the Rector's, and Mrs Challenger rescued him; she's bathing his ear. We're waiting to thank her. You needn't—

THE MAID
[Eyeing them] No.

[She turns and goes out.

THE SQUIRE
Phew! What a gorgon! I say, Rector, did you really know a Challenger in the 'nineties?

THE RECTOR [Wiping his brow]
No.

THE SQUIRE
Ha! Jolly good!

LADY ELLA
Well, you see!—it's all right.

THE RECTOR
Yes, indeed. A great relief!

LADY ELLA [Moving to the door]
I must go in now.

THE SQUIRE
Hold on! You goin' to ask 'em to—to—anything?

LADY ELLA
Yes.

MAUD
I shouldn't.

LADY ELLA
Why not? We all like the look of her.

THE RECTOR
I think we should punish ourselves for entertaining that uncharitable thought.

LADY ELLA
Yes. It's horrible not having the courage to take people as they are.

THE SQUIRE
As they are? H'm! How can you till you know?

LADY ELLA
Trust our instincts, of course.

THE SQUIRE
And supposing she'd turned out not married—eh!

LADY ELLA
She'd still be herself, wouldn't she?

MAUD
Ella!

THE SQUIRE
H'm! Don't know about that.

LADY ELLA
Of course she would, Tommy.

THE RECTOR [His hand stealing to his waist]
Well! It's a great weight off my—!

LADY ELLA
There's the poor darling snuffling. I must go in.

[She knocks on the door. It is opened, and **EDWARD** comes out briskly, with a neat little white pointed ear-cap on one ear.

LADY ELLA
Precious!

[**SHE HERSELF** Comes out, now properly dressed in flax-blue linen.

LADY ELLA
How perfectly sweet of you to make him that!

SHE
He's such a dear. And the other poor dog?

MAUD
Quite safe, thanks to your strop.

[**HANNIBAL** appears at the window, with the broken strop dangling. Following her gaze, they turn and see him.

MAUD
Oh! There, he's broken it. Bertie!

SHE
Let me!

[She seizes **HANNIBAL**.

THE SQUIRE
We're really most tremendously obliged to you. Afraid we've been an awful nuisance.

SHE
Not a bit. I love dogs.

THE SQUIRE
Hope to make the acquaintance of Mr—of your husband.

LADY ELLA [To **EDWARD**, who is straining]
Gently, darling! Tommy, take him.

[**THE SQUIRE** does so.

MAUD [Approaching **HANNIBAL**]
Is he behaving?

[She stops short, and her face suddenly shoots forward at **HER** hands that are holding **HANNIBAL'S** neck.

SHE
Oh! yes—he's a love.

MAUD [Regaining her upright position, and pursing her lips; in a peculiar voice]
Bertie, take Hannibal.

[**THE RECTOR** takes him.

LADY ELLA [Producing a card]
I can't be too grateful for all you've done for my poor darling. This is where we live. Do come—and see—

[**MAUD**, whose eyes have never left those hands, tweaks **LADY ELLA's** dress.

LADY ELLA
That is—I'm—I—

[**HERSELF** looks at **LADY ELLA** in surprise.

THE SQUIRE
I don't know if your husband shoots, but if—

[**MAUD**, catching his eye, taps the third finger of her left hand.]

THE SQUIRE
—er—he—does—er—er—

[**HERSELF** looks at **THE SQUIRE** surprised.

MAUD [Turning to her husband, repeats the gesture with the low and simple word]
Look!

THE RECTOR [With round eyes, severely]
Hannibal!

[He lifts him bodily and carries him away.

MAUD
Don't squeeze him, Bertie!

[She follows through the French window.

THE SQUIRE [Abruptly—of the unoffending **EDWARD**]
That dog'll be forgettin' himself in a minute.

[He picks up **EDWARD** and takes him out.

[**LADY ELLA** is left staring.

LADY ELLA [At last]
You mustn't think, I—You mustn't think, we—Oh! I must just see they—don't let Edward get at Hannibal.

[She skims away.

[**HERSELF** is left staring after **LADY ELLA**, in surprise.

SHE
What is the matter with them?

[The door is opened.

THE MAID [Entering and holding out a wedding-ring—severely]
You left this, m'm, in the bathroom.

SHE
[Looking, startled, at her finger] Oh! [Taking it] I hadn't missed it. Thank you, Martha.

[THE **MAID** goes.

[A hand, slipping in at the casement window, softly lays a pair of braces on the windowsill. SHE looks at the braces, then at the ring. **HER** lip curls.]

SHE [Murmuring deeply]
Ah!

CURTAIN

DEFEAT

A TINY DRAMA

CHARACTERS
THE OFFICER.
THE GIRL.

SCENE
During the Great War. Evening.

DEFEAT

An empty room. The curtains drawn and gas turned low. The furniture and walls give a colour-impression as of greens and beetroot. There is a prevalence of plush. A fireplace on the Left, a sofa, a small table; the curtained window is at the back. On the table, in a common pot, stands a little plant of maidenhair fern, fresh and green.

Enter from the door on the Right, a **GIRL** and a **YOUNG OFFICER** in khaki. The **GIRL** wears a discreet dark dress, hat, and veil, and stained yellow gloves. The **YOUNG OFFICER** is tall, with a fresh open face, and kindly eager blue eyes; he is a little lame. The **GIRL**, who is evidently at home, moves towards the gas jet to turn it up, then changes her mind, and going to the curtains, draws them apart and throws up the window. Bright moonlight comes flooding in. Outside are seen the trees of a little Square. She stands gazing out, suddenly turns inward with a shiver.

YOUNG OFFICER
I say; what's the matter? You were crying when I spoke to you.

GIRL [With a movement of recovery]
Oh! nothing. The beautiful evening-that's all.

YOUNG OFFICER [Looking at her]
Cheer up!

GIRL [Taking of hat and veil; her hair is yellowish and crinkly]
Cheer up! You are not lonelee, like me.

YOUNG OFFICER [Limping to the window—doubtfully]
I say, how did you how did you get into this? Isn't it an awfully hopeless sort of life?

GIRL
Yees, it ees. You haf been wounded?

YOUNG OFFICER
Just out of hospital to-day.

GIRL
The horrible war—all the misery is because of the war. When will it end?

YOUNG OFFICER [Leaning against the window-sill, looking at her attentively]
I say, what nationality are you?

GIRL [With a quick look and away]
Rooshian.

YOUNG OFFICER
Really! I never met a Russian girl.

[The **GIRL** gives him another quick look.

I say, is it as bad as they make out?

GIRL [Slipping her hand through his arm]
Not when I haf anyone as ni-ice as you; I never haf had, though. [She smiles, and her smile, like her speech, is slow and confining] You stopped because I was sad, others stop because I am gay. I am not fond of men at all. When you know—you are not fond of them.

YOUNG OFFICER
Well, you hardly know them at their best, do you? You should see them in the trenches. By George! They're simply splendid—officers and men, every blessed soul. There's never been anything like it—just one long bit of jolly fine self-sacrifice; it's perfectly amazing.

GIRL [Turning her blue-grey eyes on him]
I expect you are not the last at that. You see in them what you haf in yourself, I think.

YOUNG OFFICER

Oh, not a bit; you're quite out! I assure you when we made the attack where I got wounded there wasn't a single man in my regiment who wasn't an absolute hero. The way they went in—never thinking of themselves—it was simply ripping.

GIRL [In a queer voice]
It is the same too, perhaps, with—the enemy.

YOUNG OFFICER
Oh, yes! I know that.

GIRL
Ah! You are not a mean man. How I hate mean men!

YOUNG OFFICER
Oh! they're not mean really—they simply don't understand.

GIRL
Oh! You are a babee—a good babee aren't you?

[The **YOUNG OFFICER** doesn't like this, and frowns. The **GIRL** looks a little scared.

GIRL [Clingingly]
But I li-ke you for it. It is so good to find a ni-ice man.

YOUNG OFFICER [Abruptly]
About being lonely? Haven't you any Russian friends?

GIRL [Blankly]
Rooshian? No. [Quickly] The town is so beeg. Were you at the concert before you spoke to me?

YOUNG OFFICER
Yes.

GIRL
I too. I lofe music.

YOUNG OFFICER
I suppose all Russians do.

GIRL [With another quick look tat him]
I go there always when I haf the money.

YOUNG OFFICER
What! Are you as badly on the rocks as that?

GIRL
Well, I haf just one shilling now!

[She laughs bitterly. The laugh upsets him; he sits on the window-sill, and leans forward towards her.

YOUNG OFFICER
I say, what's your name?

GIRL
May. Well, I call myself that. It is no good asking yours.

YOUNG OFFICER [With a laugh]
You're a distrustful little soul; aren't you?

GIRL
I haf reason to be, don't you think?

YOUNG OFFICER
Yes. I suppose you're bound to think us all brutes.

GIRL [Sitting on a chair close to the window where the moonlight falls on one powdered cheek]
Well, I haf a lot of reasons to be afraid all my time. I am dreadfully nervous now; I am not trusding anybody. I suppose you haf been killing lots of Germans?

YOUNG OFFICER
We never know, unless it happens to be hand to hand; I haven't come in for that yet.

GIRL
But you would be very glad if you had killed some.

YOUNG OFFICER
Oh, glad? I don't think so. We're all in the same boat, so far as that's concerned. We're not glad to kill each other—not most of us. We do our job—that's all.

GIRL
Oh! It is frightful. I expect I haf my brothers killed.

YOUNG OFFICER
Don't you get any news ever?

GIRL
News? No indeed, no news of anybody in my country. I might not haf a country; all that I ever knew is gone; fader, moder, sisters, broders, all; never any more I shall see them, I suppose, now. The war it breaks and breaks, it breaks hearts. [She gives a little snarl] Do you know what I was thinking when you came up to me? I was thinking of my native town, and the river in the moonlight. If I could see it again I would be glad. Were you ever homeseeck?

YOUNG OFFICER
Yes, I have been—in the trenches. But one's ashamed with all the others.

GIRL

Ah! Yees! Yees! You are all comrades there. What is it like for me here, do you think, where everybody hates and despises me, and would catch me and put me in prison, perhaps. [Her breast heaves.]

YOUNG OFFICER [Leaning forward and patting her knee]
Sorry—sorry.

GIRL [In a smothered voice]
You are the first who has been kind to me for so long! I will tell you the truth—I am not Rooshian at all—I am German.

YOUNG OFFICER [Staring]
My dear girl, who cares. We aren't fighting against women.

GIRL [Peering at him]
Another man said that to me. But he was thinkin' of his fun. You are a veree ni-ice boy; I am so glad I met you. You see the good in people, don't you? That is the first thing in the world—because—there is really not much good in people, you know.

YOUNG OFFICER [Smiling]
You are a dreadful little cynic! But of course you are!

GIRL
Cyneec? How long do you think I would live if I was not a cyneec? I should drown myself to-morrow. Perhaps there are good people, but, you see, I don't know them.

YOUNG OFFICER
I know lots.

GIRL [Leaning towards him]
Well now—see, ni-ice boy—you haf never been in a hole, haf you?

YOUNG OFFICER
I suppose not a real hole.

GIRL
No, I should think not, with your face. Well, suppose I am still a good girl, as I was once, you know; and you took me to your mother and your sisters and you said: "Here is a little German girl that has no work, and no money, and no friends." They will say: "Oh! how sad! A German girl!" And they will go and wash their hands.

[The **OFFICER**, is silent, staring at her.

GIRL
You see.

YOUNG OFFICER [Muttering]
I'm sure there are people.

GIRL

No. They would not take a German, even if she was good. Besides, I don't want to be good any more—I am not a humbug; I have learned to be bad. Aren't you going to kees me, ni-ice boy?

[She puts her face close to his. Her eyes trouble him; he draws back.

YOUNG OFFICER

Don't. I'd rather not, if you don't mind. [She looks at him fixedly, with a curious inquiring stare] It's stupid. I don't know—but you see, out there, and in hospital, life's different. It's—it's—it isn't mean, you know. Don't come too close.

GIRL

Oh! You are fun—[She stops] Eesn't it light. No Zeps to-night. When they burn—what a 'orrble death! And all the people cheer. It is natural. Do you hate us veree much?

YOUNG OFFICER [Turning sharply]

Hate? I don't know.

GIRL

I don't hate even the English—I despise them. I despise my people too; even more, because they began this war. Oh! I know that. I despise all the peoples. Why haf they made the world so miserable—why haf they killed all our lives—hundreds and thousands and millions of lives—all for noting? They haf made a bad world—everybody hating, and looking for the worst everywhere. They haf made me bad, I know. I believe no more in anything. What is there to believe in? Is there a God? No! Once I was teaching little English children their prayers—isn't that funnee? I was reading to them about Christ and love. I believed all those things. Now I believe noting at all—no one who is not a fool or a liar can believe. I would like to work in a 'ospital; I would like to go and 'elp poor boys like you. Because I am a German they would throw me out a 'undred times, even if I was good. It is the same in Germany, in France, in Russia, everywhere. But do you think I will believe in Love and Christ and God and all that— Not I! I think we are animals—that's all! Oh, yes! you fancy it is because my life has spoiled me. It is not that at all—that is not the worst thing in life. The men I take are not ni-ice, like you, but it's their nature; and—they help me to live, which is something for me, anyway. No, it is the men who think themselves great and good and make the war with their talk and their hate, killing us all—killing all the boys like you, and keeping poor People in prison, and telling us to go on hating; and all these dreadful cold-blood creatures who write in the papers—the same in my country—just the same; it is because of all of them that I think we are only animals.

[The **YOUNG OFFICER** gets up, acutely miserable.

[She follows him with her eyes.

GIRL

Don't mind me talkin', ni-ice boy. I don't know anyone to talk to. If you don't like it, I can be quiet as a mouse.

YOUNG OFFICER

Oh, go on! Talk away; I'm not obliged to believe you, and I don't.

[She, too, is on her feet now, leaning against the wall; her dark dress and white face just touched by the slanting moonlight. Her voice comes again, slow and soft and bitter.

GIRL

Well, look here, ni-ice boy, what sort of world is it, where millions are being tortured, for no fault of theirs, at all? A beautiful world, isn't it? 'Umbog! Silly rot, as you boys call it. You say it is all "Comrades" and braveness out there at the front, and people don't think of themselves. Well, I don't think of myself veree much. What does it matter? I am lost now, anyway. But I think of my people at 'ome; how they suffer and grieve. I think of all the poor people there, and here, how lose those they love, and all the poor prisoners. Am I not to think of them? And if I do, how am I to believe it a beautiful world, ni-ice boy?

[He stands very still, staring at her.

GIRL

Look here! We haf one life each, and soon it is over. Well, I think that is lucky.

YOUNG OFFICER

No! There's more than that.

GIRL [Softly]

Ah! You think the war is fought for the future; you are giving your lives for a better world, aren't you?

YOUNG OFFICER

We must fight till we win.

GIRL

Till you win. My people think that too. All the peoples think that if they win the world will be better. But it will not, you know; it will be much worse, anyway.

[He turns away from her, and catches up his cap. Her voice follows him.

GIRL

I don't care which win. I don't care if my country is beaten. I despise them all—animals—animals. Ah! Don't go, ni-ice boy; I will be quiet now.

[He has taken some notes from his tunic pocket; he puts then on the table and goes up to her.

YOUNG OFFICER

Good-night.

GIRL [Plaintively]

Are you really going? Don't you like me enough?

YOUNG OFFICER

Yes, I like you.

GIRL

It is because I am German, then?

YOUNG OFFICER
No.

GIRL
Then why won't you stay?

YOUNG OFFICER [With a shrug]
If you must know—because you upset me.

GIRL
Won't you kees me once?

[He bends, puts his lips to her forehead. But as he takes them away she throws her head back, presses her mouth to his, and clings to him.

YOUNG OFFICER [Sitting down suddenly]
Don't! I don't want to feel a brute.

GIRL [Laughing]
You are a funny boy; but you are veree good. Talk to me a little, then. No one talks to me. Tell me, haf you seen many German prisoners?

YOUNG OFFICER [Sighing]
A good many.

GIRL
Any from the Rhine?

YOUNG OFFICER
Yes, I think so.

GIRL
Were they veree sad?

YOUNG OFFICER
Some were; some were quite glad to be taken.

GIRL
Did you ever see the Rhine? It will be wonderful to-night. The moonlight will be the same there, and in Rooshia too, and France, everywhere; and the trees will look the same as here, and people will meet under them and make love just as here. Oh! isn't it stupid, the war? As if it were not good to be alive!

YOUNG OFFICER
You can't tell how good it is to be alive till you're facing death. You don't live till then. And when a whole lot of you feel like that—and are ready to give their lives for each other, it's worth all the rest of life put together.

[He stops, ashamed of such, sentiment before this girl, who believes in nothing.]

GIRL [Softly]
How were you wounded, ni-ice boy?

YOUNG OFFICER
Attacking across open ground: four machine bullets got me at one go off.

GIRL
Weren't you veree frightened when they ordered you to attack?

[He shakes his head and laughs.

YOUNG OFFICER
It was great. We did laugh that morning. They got me much too soon, though—a swindle.

GIRL [Staring at him]
You laughed?

YOUNG OFFICER
Yes. And what do you think was the first thing I was conscious of next morning? My old Colonel bending over me and giving me a squeeze of lemon. If you knew my Colonel you'd still believe in things. There is something, you know, behind all this evil. After all, you can only die once, and, if it's for your country—all the better!

[Her face, in the moonlight, with, intent eyes touched up with black, has a most strange, other-world look.

GIRL
No; I believe in nothing, not even in my country. My heart is dead.

YOUNG OFFICER
Yes; you think so, but it isn't, you know, or you wouldn't have 'been crying when I met you.

GIRL
If it were not dead, do you think I could live my life-walking the streets every night, pretending to like strange men; never hearing a kind word; never talking, for fear I will be known for a German? Soon I shall take to drinking; then I shall be "Kaput" veree quick. You see, I am practical; I see things clear. To-night I am a little emotional; the moon is funny, you know. But I live for myself only, now. I don't care for anything or anybody.

YOUNG OFFICER
All the same; just now you were pitying your folk at home, and prisoners and that.

GIRL

Yees; because they suffer. Those who suffer are like me—I pity myself, that's all; I am different from your English women. I see what I am doing; I do not let my mind become a turnip just because I am no longer moral.

YOUNG OFFICER
Nor your heart either, for all you say.

GIRL
Ni-ice boy, you are veree obstinate. But all that about love is 'umbog. We love ourselves, noting more.

[At that intense soft bitterness in her voice, he gets up, feeling stifled, and stands at the window. A newspaper **BOY** some way off is calling his wares. The **GIRL's** fingers slip between his own, and stay unmoving. He looks round into her face. In spite of make-up it has a queer, unholy, touching beauty.

YOUNG OFFICER [With an outburst]
No; we don't only love ourselves; there is more. I can't explain, but there's something great; there's kindness—and—and—-

[The shouting of newspaper **BOYS** grows louder and their cries, passionately vehement, clash into each other and obscure each word. His head goes up to listen; her hand tightens within his arm—she too is listening. The cries come nearer, hoarser, more shrill and clamorous; the empty moonlight outside seems suddenly crowded with figures, footsteps, voices, and a fierce distant cheering. "Great victory— great victory! Official! British! 'Eavy defeat of the 'Uns! Many thousand prisoners! 'Eavy defeat!" It speeds by, intoxicating, filling him with a fearful joy; he leans far out, waving his cap and cheering like a madman; the night seems to flutter and vibrate and answer. He turns to rush down into the street, strikes against something soft, and recoils. The **GIRL** stands with hands clenched, and face convulsed, panting. All confused with the desire to do something, he stoops to kiss her hand. She snatches away her fingers, sweeps up the notes he has put down, and holds them out to him.

GIRL
Take them—I will not haf your English money—take them.

[Suddenly she tears them across, twice, thrice, lets the bits flutter to the floor, and turns her back on him. He stands looking at her leaning against the plush-covered table, her head down, a dark figure in a dark room, with the moonlight sharpening her outline. Hardly a moment he stays, then makes for the door. When he is gone, she still stands there, her chin on her breast, with the sound in her ears of cheering, of hurrying feet, and voices crying: "'Eavy Defeat!" stands, in the centre of a pattern made by the fragments of the torn-up notes, staring out unto the moonlight, seeing not this hated room and the hated Square outside, but a German orchard, and herself, a little girl, plucking apples, a big dog beside her; and a hundred other pictures, such as the drowning see. Then she sinks down on the floor, lays her forehead on the dusty carpet, and presses her body to it. Mechanically, she sweeps together the scattered fragments of notes, assembling them with the dust into a little pile, as of fallen leaves, and dabbling in it with her fingers, while the tears run down her cheeks.

GIRL
Defeat! Der Vaterland! Defeat! . . . One shillin'!

[Then suddenly, in the moonlight, she sits up, and begins to sing with all her might "Die Wacht am Rhein." And outside men pass, singing: "Rule, Britannia!"

CURTAIN

THE SUN

A SCENE

CHARACTERS
THE GIRL.
THE MAN.
THE SOLDIER.

THE SUN

A **GIRL**, sits crouched over her knees on a stile close to a river. **A MAN** with a silver badge stands beside her, clutching the worn top plank. **THE GIRL'S** level brows are drawn together; her eyes see her memories. **THE MAN's** eyes see **THE GIRL**; he has a dark, twisted face. The bright sun shines; the quiet river flows; the Cuckoo is calling; the mayflower is in bloom along the hedge that ends in the stile on the towing-path.

THE GIRL
God knows what 'e'll say, Jim.

THE MAN
Let 'im. 'E's come too late, that's all.

THE GIRL
He couldn't come before. I'm frightened. 'E was fond o' me.

THE MAN
And aren't I fond of you?

THE GIRL
I ought to 'a waited, Jim; with 'im in the fightin'.

THE MAN [Passionately]
And what about me? Aren't I been in the fightin'—earned all I could get?

THE GIRL [Touching him]
Ah!

THE MAN
Did you—?

[He cannot speak the words.

THE GIRL
Not like you, Jim—not like you.

THE MAN
Have a spirit, then.

THE GIRL
I promised him.

THE MAN
One man's luck's another's poison.

THE GIRL
I ought to 'a waited. I never thought he'd come back from the fightin'.

THE MAN [Grimly]
Maybe 'e'd better not 'ave.

THE GIRL [Looking back along the tow-path]
What'll he be like, I wonder?

THE MAN [Gripping her shoulder]
Daisy, don't you never go back on me, or I should kill you, and 'im too.

[**THE GIRL** looks at him, shivers, and puts her lips to his.

THE GIRL
I never could.

THE MAN
Will you run for it? 'E'd never find us!

[**THE GIRL** shakes her head.

THE MAN [Dully]
What's the good o' stayin'? The world's wide.

THE GIRL
I'd rather have it off me mind, with him home.

THE MAN [Clenching his hands]
It's temptin' Providence.

THE GIRL
What's the time, Jim?

THE MAN [Glancing at the sun]

'Alf past four.

THE GIRL [Looking along the towing-path]

He said four o'clock. Jim, you better go.

THE MAN

Not I. I've not got the wind up. I've seen as much of hell as he has, any day. What like is he?

THE GIRL [Dully]

I dunno, just. I've not seen him these three years. I dunno no more, since I've known you.

THE MAN

Big or little chap?

THE GIRL

'Bout your size. Oh! Jim, go along!

THE MAN

No fear! What's a blighter like that to old Fritz's shells? We didn't shift when they was comin'. If you'll go, I'll go; not else.

[Again she shakes her head.

THE GIRL

Jim, do you love me true?

[For answer **THE MAN** takes her avidly in his arms.

I ain't ashamed—I ain't ashamed. If 'e could see me 'eart.

THE MAN

Daisy! If I'd known you out there, I never could 'a stuck it. They'd 'a got me for a deserter. That's how I love you!

THE GIRL

Jim, don't lift your hand to 'im! Promise!

THE MAN

That's according.

THE GIRL

Promise!

THE MAN

If 'e keeps quiet, I won't. But I'm not accountable—not always, I tell you straight—not since I've been through that.

THE GIRL [With a shiver]
Nor p'raps he isn't.

THE MAN
Like as not. It takes the lynch pins out, I tell you.

THE GIRL
God 'elp us!

THE MAN [Grimly]
Ah! We said that a bit too often. What we want we take, now; there's no one else to give it us, and there's no fear'll stop us; we seen the bottom of things.

THE GIRL
P'raps he'll say that too.

THE MAN
Then it'll be 'im or me.

THE GIRL
I'm frightened:

THE MAN [Tenderly]
No, Daisy, no! The river's handy. One more or less. 'E shan't 'arm you; nor me neither.

[He takes out a knife.

THE GIRL [Seizing his hand]
Oh, no! Give it to me, Jim!

THE MAN [Smiling]
No fear! [He puts it away] Shan't 'ave no need for it like as not. All right, little Daisy; you can't be expected to see things like what we do. What's life, anyway? I've seen a thousand lives taken in five minutes. I've seen dead men on the wires like flies on a flypaper. I've been as good as dead meself a hundred times. I've killed a dozen men. It's nothin'. He's safe, if 'e don't get my blood up. If he does, nobody's safe; not 'im, nor anybody else; not even you. I'm speakin' sober.

THE GIRL [Softly]
Jim, you won't go fightin' in the sun, with the birds all callin'?

THE MAN
That depends on 'im. I'm not lookin' for it. Daisy, I love you. I love your hair. I love your eyes. I love you.

THE GIRL
And I love you, Jim. I don't want nothin' more than you in all the world.

THE MAN
Amen to that, my dear. Kiss me close!

The sound of a voice singing breaks in on their embrace. **THE GIRL** starts from his arms, and looks behind her along the towing-path. **THE MAN** draws back against, the hedge, fingering his side, where the knife is hidden. The song comes nearer.

"I'll be right there to-night,
Where the fields are snowy white;
Banjos ringing, darkies singing,
All the world seems bright."

THE GIRL
It's him!

THE MAN
Don't get the wind up, Daisy. I'm here!

[The singing stops. **A MAN'S VOICE** says "Christ! It's Daisy; it's little Daisy 'erself!" **THE GIRL** stands rigid. The figure of a **SOLDIER** appears on the other side of the stile. His cap is tucked into his belt, his hair is bright in the sunshine; he is lean, wasted, brown, and laughing.]

SOLDIER
Daisy! Daisy! Hallo, old pretty girl!

[**THE GIRL** does not move, barring the way, as it were.

THE GIRL
Hallo, Jack! [Softly] I got things to tell you!

SOLDIER
What sort o' things, this lovely day? Why, I got things that'd take me years to tell. Have you missed me, Daisy?

THE GIRL
You been so long.

SOLDIER
So I 'ave. My Gawd! It's a way they 'ave in the Army. I said when I got out of it I'd laugh. Like as the sun itself I used to think of you, Daisy, when the trumps was comin' over, and the wind was up. D'you remember that last night in the wood? "Come back and marry me quick, Jack." Well, here I am—got me pass to heaven. No more fightin', no more drillin', no more sleepin' rough. We can get married now, Daisy. We can live soft an' 'appy. Give us a kiss, my dear.

THE GIRL [Drawing back]
No.

SOLDIER [Blankly]

Why not?

[**THE MAN**, with a swift movement steps along the hedge to **THE GIRL**'S side.

THE MAN
That's why, soldier.

SOLDIER [Leaping over the stile]
'Oo are you, Pompey? The sun don't shine in your inside, do it? 'Oo is he, Daisy?

THE GIRL
My man.

SOLDIER
Your-man! Lummy! "Taffy was a Welshman, Taffy was a thief!" Well, mate! So you've been through it, too. I'm laughin' this mornin' as luck will 'ave it. Ah! I can see your knife.

THE MAN [Who has half drawn his knife]
Don't laugh at me, I tell you.

SOLDIER
Not at you, not at you. [He looks from one to the other] I'm laughin' at things in general. Where did you get it, mate?

THE MAN [Watchfully]
Through the lung.

SOLDIER
Think o' that! An' I never was touched. Four years an' never was touched. An' so you've come an' took my girl! Nothin' doin'! Ha! [Again he looks from one to the other-then away] Well! The world's before me! [He laughs] I'll give you Daisy for a lung protector.

THE MAN [Fiercely]
You won't. I've took her.

SOLDIER
That's all right, then. You keep 'er. I've got a laugh in me you can't put out, black as you look! Good-bye, little Daisy!

[**THE GIRL** makes a movement towards him.

THE MAN
Don't touch 'im!

[**THE GIRL** stands hesitating, and suddenly bursts into tears.

SOLDIER

Look 'ere, mate; shake 'ands! I don't want to see a girl cry, this day of all, with the sun shinin'. I seen too much of sorrer. You and me've been at the back of it. We've 'ad our whack. Shake!

THE MAN
Who are you kiddin'? You never loved 'er!

SOLDIER [After a long moment's pause]
Oh! I thought I did.

THE MAN
I'll fight you for her.

[He drops his knife.

SOLDIER [Slowly]
Mate, you done your bit, an' I done mine. It's took us two ways, seemin'ly.

THE GIRL [Pleading]
Jim!

THE MAN [With clenched fists]
I don't want 'is charity. I only want what I can take.

SOLDIER
Daisy, which of us will you 'ave?

THE GIRL [Covering her face]
Oh! Him!

SOLDIER
You see, mate! Put your 'ands down. There's nothin' for it but a laugh. You an' me know that. Laugh, mate!

THE MAN
You blarsted—!

[**THE GIRL** springs to him and stops his mouth.]

SOLDIER
It's no use, mate. I can't do it. I said I'd laugh to-day, and laugh I will. I've come through that, an' all the stink of it; I've come through sorrer. Never again! Cheerio, mate! The sun's a-shinin'! He turns away.

THE GIRL
Jack, don't think too 'ard of me!

SOLDIER [Looking back]
No fear, my dear! Enjoy your fancy! So long! Gawd bless you both!

He sings, and goes along the path, and the song fades away.

"I'll be right there to-night
Where the fields are snowy white;
Banjos ringing, darkies singing
All the world seems bright!"

THE MAN
'E's mad!

THE GIRL [Looking down the path with her hands clasped]
The sun has touched 'im, Jim!

CURTAIN

PUNCH AND GO

A LITTLE COMEDY

"Orpheus with his lute made trees And the mountain tope that freeze....."

PERSONS OF THE PLAY
JAMES G. FRUST - The Boss
E. BLEWITT VANE - The Producer
MR. FORESON - The Stage Manager
"ELECTRICS" - The Electrician
"PROPS" - The Property Man
HERBERT - The Call Boy

OF THE PLAY WITHIN THE PLAY
GUY TOONE - The Professor
VANESSA HELLGROVE - The Wife
GEORGE FLEETWAY - Orpheus
MAUDE HOPKINS - The Faun

SCENE: The Stage of a Theatre.

Action continuous, though the curtain is momentarily lowered according to that action.

PUNCH AND GO

The Scene is the stage of the theatre set for the dress rehearsal of the little play: "Orpheus with his Lute." The curtain is up and the audience, though present, is not supposed to be. The set scene represents the end section of a room, with wide French windows, Back Centre, fully opened on to an apple orchard in bloom. The Back Wall with these French windows, is set only about ten feet from the footlights, and the rest of the stage is orchard. What is visible of the room would indicate the study of a writing man of culture. (Note.—If found advantageous for scenic purposes, this section of room can be changed to a broad verandah or porch with pillars supporting its roof.) In the wall, Stage Left, is a curtained opening, across which the curtain is half drawn. Stage Right of the French windows is a large armchair turned rather towards the window, with a book rest attached, on which is a volume of the Encyclopedia Britannica, while on a stool alongside are writing materials such as a man requires when he writes with a pad on his knees. On a little table close by is a reading-lamp with a dark green shade. A crude light from the floats makes the stage stare; the only person on it is **MR FORESON**, the stage manager, who is standing in the centre looking upwards as if waiting for someone to speak. He is a short, broad man, rather blank, and fatal. From the back of the auditorium, or from an empty box, whichever is most convenient, the producer, **MR BLEWITT VANE**, a man of about thirty four, with his hair brushed back, speaks.

VANE
Mr Foreson?

FORESON
Sir?

VANE
We'll do that lighting again.

[**FORESON** walks straight of the Stage into the wings Right.

[A pause.]

Mr Foreson! [Crescendo] Mr Foreson.

[**FORESON** walks on again from Right and shades his eyes.

VANE
For goodness sake, stand by! We'll do that lighting again. Check your floats.

FORESON
[Speaking up into the prompt wings] Electrics!

VOICE OF ELECTRICS
Hallo!

FORESON
Give it us again. Check your floats.

[The floats go down, and there is a sudden blinding glare of blue lights, in which **FORESON** looks particularly ghastly.

VANE
Great Scott! What the blazes! Mr Foreson!

[**FORESON** walks straight out into the wings Left. Crescendo.

Mr Foreson!

FORESON [Re-appearing]
Sir?

VANE
Tell Miller to come down.

FORESON
Electrics! Mr Blewitt Vane wants to speak to you. Come down!

VANE
Tell Herbert to sit in that chair.

[**FORESON** walks straight out into the Right wings.

Mr Foreson!

FORESON [Re-appearing]
Sir?

VANE
Don't go off the stage.

[**FORESON** mutters.

[**ELECTRICS** appears from the wings, Stage Left. He is a dark, thin-faced man with rather spikey hair.]

ELECTRICS
Yes, Mr Vane?

VANE
Look!

ELECTRICS
That's what I'd got marked, Mr Vane.

VANE
Once for all, what I want is the orchard in full moonlight, and the room dark except for the reading lamp. Cut off your front battens.

[**ELECTRICS** withdraws Left. **FORESON** walks off the Stage into the Right wings.

Mr Foreson!

FORESON [Re-appearing]
Sir?

VANE
See this marked right. Now, come on with it! I want to get some beauty into this!

[While he is speaking, **HERBERT**, the call boy, appears from the wings Right, a mercurial youth of about sixteen with a wide mouth.

FORESON [Maliciously]
Here you are, then, Mr Vane. Herbert, sit in that chair.

[**HERBERT** sits an the armchair, with an air of perfect peace.

VANE
Now! [All the lights go out. In a wail] Great Scott!

[A throaty chuckle from **FORESON** in the darkness. The light dances up, flickers, shifts, grows steady, falling on the orchard outside. The reading lamp darts alight and a piercing little glare from it strikes into the auditorium away from **HERBERT**.

[In a terrible voice] Mr Foreson.

FORESON
Sir?

VANE
Look—at—that—shade!

[**FORESON** mutters, walks up to it and turns it round so that the light shines on **HERBERT'S** legs.]

On his face, on his face!

[**FORESON** turns the light accordingly.]

FORESON
Is that what you want, Mr Vane?

VANE
Yes. Now, mark that!

FORESON [Up into wings Right]
Electrics!

ELECTRICS

Hallo!

FORESON
Mark that!

VANE
My God!

[The blue suddenly becomes amber.

[The blue returns. All is steady. **HERBERT** is seen diverting himself with an imaginary cigar.

Mr Foreson.

FORESON
Sir?

VANE
Ask him if he's got that?

FORESON
Have you got that?

ELECTRICS
Yes.

VANE
Now pass to the change. Take your floats off altogether.

FORESON [Calling up]
Floats out. [They go out.]

VANE
Cut off that lamp.

[The lamp goes out.

Put a little amber in your back batten. Mark that! Now pass to the end. Mr Foreson!

FORESON
Sir?

VANE
Black out

FORESON [Calling up]
Black out!

[The lights go out.

VANE
Give us your first lighting-lamp on. And then the two changes. Quick as you can. Put some pep into it.
Mr Foreson!

FORESON
Sir?

VANE
Stand for me where Miss Hellgrove comes in.

[**FORESON** crosses to the window.

No, no!—by the curtain.

[**FORESON** takes his stand by the curtain; and suddenly the three lighting effects are rendered quickly
and with miraculous exactness.]

Good! Leave it at that. We'll begin. Mr Foreson, send up to Mr Frust.

[He moves from the auditorium and ascends on to the Stage, by some steps Stage Right.

FORESON
Herb! Call the boss, and tell beginners to stand by. Sharp, now!

[**HERBERT** gets out of the chair, and goes off Right.

[**FORESON** is going off Left as **VANE** mounts the Stage.

VANE
Mr Foreson.

FORESON [Re-appearing]
Sir?

VANE
I want "Props."

FORESON [In a stentorian voice]
"Props!"

[Another moth-eaten **MAN** appears through the French windows.

VANE
Is that boulder firm?

PROPS [Going to where, in front of the back-cloth, and apparently among its apple trees, lies the counterfeitment of a mossy boulder; he puts his foot on it]
If, you don't put too much weight on it, sir.

VANE
It won't creak?

PROPS
Nao.

[He mounts on it, and a dolorous creaking arises.

VANE
Make that right. Let me see that lute.

[**PROPS** produces a property lute. While they scrutinize it, a broad man with broad leathery clean-shaven face and small mouth, occupied by the butt end of a cigar, has come on to the stage from Stage Left, and stands waiting to be noticed.

PROPS [Attracted by the scent of the cigar]
The Boss, Sir.

VANE [Turning to "**PROPS**"]
That'll do, then.

["**PROPS**" goes out through the French windows.

VANE [To **FRUST**]
Now, sir, we're all ready for rehearsal of "Orpheus with his Lute."

FRUST [In a cosmopolitan voice]
"Orphoos with his loot!" That his loot, Mr Vane? Why didn't he pinch something more precious? Has this high-brow curtain-raiser of yours got any "pep" in it?

VANE
It has charm.

FRUST
I'd thought of "Pop goes the Weasel" with little Miggs. We kind of want a cock-tail before "Louisa loses," Mr Vane.

VANE
Well, sir, you'll see.

FRUST
This your lighting? It's a bit on the spiritool side. I've left my glass. Guess I'll sit in the front row. Ha'f a minute. Who plays this Orphoos?

VANE
George Fleetway.

FRUST
Has he got punch?

VANE
It's a very small part.

FRUST
Who are the others?

VANE
Guy Toone plays the Professor; Vanessa Hellgrove his wife; Maude Hopkins the faun.

FRUST
H'm! Names don't draw.

VANE
They're not expensive, any of them. Miss Hellgrove's a find, I think.

FRUST
Pretty?

VANE
Quite.

FRUST
Arty?

VANE [Doubtfully]
No. [With resolution] Look here, Mr Frust, it's no use your expecting another "Pop goes the Weasel."

FRUST
We-ell, if it's got punch and go, that'll be enough for me. Let's get to it!

[He extinguishes his cigar and descends the steps and sits in the centre of the front row of the stalls.

VANE
Mr Foreson?

FORESON [Appearing through curtain, Right]
Sir?

VANE
Beginners. Take your curtain down.

[He descends the steps and seats himself next to **FRUST.** The curtain goes down.

[A **WOMAN'S VOICE** is heard singing very beautifully Sullivan's song: "Orpheus with his lute, with his lute made trees and the mountain tops that freeze'." etc.

FRUST
Some voice!

The curtain rises. In the armchair the **PROFESSOR** is yawning, tall, thin, abstracted, and slightly grizzled in the hair. He has a pad of paper over his knee, ink on the stool to his right and the Encyclopedia volume on the stand to his left-barricaded in fact by the article he is writing. He is reading a page over to himself, but the words are drowned in the sound of the song his WIFE is singing in the next room, partly screened off by the curtain. She finishes, and stops. His voice can then be heard conning the words of his article.

PROFESSOR
"Orpheus symbolized the voice of Beauty, the call of life, luring us mortals with his song back from the graves we dig for ourselves. Probably the ancients realized this neither more nor less than we moderns. Mankind has not changed. The civilized being still hides the faun and the dryad within its broadcloth and its silk. And yet"—

[He stops, with a dried-up air-rather impatiently]

Go on, my dear! It helps the atmosphere.

[The voice of his **WIFE** begins again, gets as far as "made them sing" and stops dead, just as the **PROFESSOR's** pen is beginning to scratch. And suddenly, drawing the curtain further aside,

[**SHE** appears. Much younger than the **PROFESSOR**, pale, very pretty, of a Botticellian type in face, figure, and in her clinging cream-coloured frock. She gazes at her abstracted husband; then swiftly moves to the lintel of the open window, and stands looking out.]

THE WIFE
God! What beauty!

PROFESSOR [Looking Up]
Umm?

THE WIFE
I said: God! What beauty!

PROFESSOR
Aha!

THE WIFE [Looking at him]
Do you know that I have to repeat everything to you nowadays?

PROFESSOR
What?

THE WIFE
That I have to repeat—

PROFESSOR
Yes; I heard. I'm sorry. I get absorbed.

THE WIFE
In all but me.

PROFESSOR [Startled]
My dear, your song was helping me like anything to get the mood. This paper is the very deuce—to balance between the historical and the natural.

THE WIFE
Who wants the natural?

PROFESSOR [Grumbling]
Umm! Wish I thought that! Modern taste! History may go hang; they're all for tuppence-coloured sentiment nowadays.

THE WIFE [As if to herself]
Is the Spring sentiment?

PROFESSOR
I beg your pardon, my dear; I didn't catch.

WIFE [As if against her will—urged by some pent-up force]
Beauty, beauty!

PROFESSOR
That's what I'm trying to say here. The Orpheus legend symbolizes to this day the call of Beauty! [He takes up his pen, while she continues to stare out at the moonlight. Yawning] Dash it! I get so sleepy; I wish you'd tell them to make the after-dinner coffee twice as strong.

WIFE
I will.

PROFESSOR
How does this strike you? [Conning] "Many Renaissance pictures, especially those of Botticelli, Francesca and Piero di Cosimo were inspired by such legends as that of Orpheus, and we owe a tiny gem—like Raphael 'Apollo and Marsyas' to the same Pagan inspiration."

WIFE
We owe it more than that—rebellion against the dry-as-dust.

PROFESSOR

Quite. I might develop that: "We owe it our revolt against the academic; or our disgust at 'big business,' and all the grossness of commercial success. We owe—". [His voice peters out.]

WIFE
It—love.

PROFESSOR [Abstracted]
Eh!

WIFE
I said: We owe it love.

PROFESSOR [Rather startled]
Possibly. But—er [With a dry smile] I mustn't say that here—hardly!

WIFE [To herself and the moonlight]
Orpheus with his lute!

PROFESSOR
Most people think a lute is a sort of flute. [Yawning heavily] My dear, if you're not going to sing again, d'you mind sitting down? I want to concentrate.

WIFE
I'm going out.

PROFESSOR
Mind the dew!

WIFE
The Christian virtues and the dew.

PROFESSOR [With a little dry laugh]
Not bad! Not bad! The Christian virtues and the dew. [His hand takes up his pen, his face droops over his paper, while his wife looks at him with a very strange face] "How far we can trace the modern resurgence against the Christian virtues to the symbolic figures of Orpheus, Pan, Apollo, and Bacchus might be difficult to estimate, but—"

[During those words his **WIFE** has passed through the window into the moonlight, and her voice rises, singing as she goes: "Orpheus with his lute, with his lute made trees . . ."

PROFESSOR [Suddenly aware of something]
She'll get her throat bad.

[He is silent as the voice swells in the distance.

Sounds queer at night-H'm!

[He is silent—Yawning. The voice dies away. Suddenly his head nods; he fights his drowsiness; writes a word or two, nods again, and in twenty seconds is asleep.

[The Stage is darkened by a black-out. **FRUST's** voice is heard speaking.

FRUST
What's that girl's name?

VANE
Vanessa Hellgrove.

FRUST
Aha!

[The Stage is lighted up again. Moonlight bright on the orchard; the room in darkness where the **PROFESSOR'S** figure is just visible sleeping in the chair, and screwed a little more round towards the window. From behind the mossy boulder a faun-like figure uncurls itself and peeps over with ears standing up and elbows leaning on the stone, playing a rustic pipe; and there are seen two rabbits and a fox sitting up and listening. A shiver of wind passes, blowing petals from the apple-trees.

[The **FAUN** darts his head towards where, from Right, comes slowly the figure of a Greek youth, holding a lute or lyre which his fingers strike, lifting out little wandering strains as of wind whinnying in funnels and odd corners. The **FAUN** darts down behind the stone, and the youth stands by the boulder playing his lute. Slowly while he plays the whitened trunk of an apple-tree is seen, to dissolve into the body of a girl with bare arms and feet, her dark hair unbound, and the face of the **PROFESSOR'S WIFE** Hypnotized, she slowly sways towards him, their eyes fixed on each other, till she is quite close. Her arms go out to him, cling round his neck and, their lips meet. But as they meet there comes a gasp and the **PROFESSOR** with rumpled hair is seen starting from his chair, his hands thrown up; and at his horrified "Oh!" the Stage is darkened with a black-out.

[The voice of **FRUST** is heard speaking.

FRUST
Gee!

[The Stage is lighted up again, as in the opening scene. The **PROFESSOR** is seen in his chair, with spilt sheets of paper round him, waking from a dream. He shakes himself, pinches his leg, stares heavily round into the moonlight, rises.

PROFESSOR
Phew! Beastly dream! Boof! H'm! [He moves to the window and calls.] Blanche! Blanche! [To himself] Made trees-made trees! [Calling] Blanche!

WIFE's VOICE
Yes.

PROFESSOR
Where are you?

WIFE [Appearing by the stone with her hair down]
Here!

PROFESSOR
I say—I—I've been asleep—had a dream. Come in. I'll tell you.

[She comes, and they stand in the window.

PROFESSOR
I dreamed I saw a-faun on that boulder blowing on a pipe. [He looks nervously at the stone] With two damned little rabbits and a fox sitting up and listening. And then from out there came our friend Orpheus playing on his confounded lute, till he actually turned that tree there into you. And gradually he-he drew you like a snake till you—er—put your arms round his neck and—er—kissed him. Boof! I woke up. Most unpleasant. Why! Your hair's down!

WIFE
Yes.

PROFESSOR
Why?

WIFE
It was no dream. He was bringing me to life.

PROFESSOR
What on earth?

WIFE
Do you suppose I am alive? I'm as dead as Euridice.

PROFESSOR
Good heavens, Blanche, what's the matter with you to-night?

WIFE [Pointing to the litter of papers]
Why don't we live, instead of writing of it? [She points out unto the moonlight] What do we get out of life? Money, fame, fashion, talk, learning? Yes. And what good are they? I want to live!

PROFESSOR [Helplessly]
My dear, I really don't know what you mean.

WIFE [Pointing out into the moonlight]
Look! Orpheus with his lute, and nobody can see him. Beauty, beauty, beauty—we let it go. [With sudden passion] Beauty, love, the spring. They should be in us, and they're all outside.

PROFESSOR
My dear, this is—this is—awful. [He tries to embrace her.]

WIFE [Avoiding him—an a stilly voice]
Oh! Go on with your writing!

PROFESSOR
I'm—I'm upset. I've never known you so—so—

WIFE
Hysterical? Well! It's over. I'll go and sing.

PROFESSOR [Soothingly]
There, there! I'm sorry, darling; I really am. You're kipped—you're kipped. [He gives and she accepts a kiss] Better?

[He gravitates towards his papers.

All right, now?

WIFE [Standing still and looking at him]
Quite!

PROFESSOR
Well, I'll try and finish this to-night; then, to-morrow we might have a jaunt. How about a theatre? There's a thing—they say—called "Chinese Chops," that's been running years.

WIFE [Softly to herself as he settles down into his chair]
Oh! God!

[While he takes up a sheet of paper and adjusts himself, she stands at the window staring with all her might at the boulder, till from behind it the faun's head and shoulders emerge once more.

PROFESSOR
Very queer the power suggestion has over the mind. Very queer! There's nothing really in animism, you know, except the curious shapes rocks, trees and things take in certain lights—effect they have on our imagination. [He looks up] What's the matter now?

WIFE [Startled]
Nothing! Nothing!

[Her eyes waver to him again, and the **FAUN** vanishes. She turns again to look at the boulder; there is nothing there; a little shiver of wind blows some petals off the trees. She catches one of them, and turning quickly, goes out through the curtain.

PROFESSOR [Coming to himself and writing]
"The Orpheus legend is the—er—apotheosis of animism. Can we accept—"

[His voice is lost in the sound of his **WIFE'S** voice beginning again: "Orpheus with his lute—with his lute made trees—" It dies in a sob. The **PROFESSOR** looks up startled, as the curtain falls.

FRUST
Fine! Fine!

VANE
Take up the curtain. Mr Foreson?

[The curtain goes up.

FORESON
Sir?

VANE
Everybody on.

[He and **FRUST** leave their seats and ascend on to the Stage, on which are collecting the four **PLAYERS**.

VANE
Give us some light.

FORESON
Electrics! Turn up your floats!

[The footlights go up, and the blue goes out; the light is crude as at the beginning.

FRUST
I'd like to meet Miss Hellgrove. [She comes forward eagerly and timidly. He grasps her hand] Miss Hellgrove, I want to say I thought that fine—fine. [Her evident emotion and pleasure warm him so that he increases his grasp and commendation] Fine. It quite got my soft spots. Emotional. Fine!

MISS HELLGROVE
Oh! Mr Frust; it means so much to me. Thank you!

FRUST [A little balder in the eye, and losing warmth]
Er—fine! [His eye wanders] Where's Mr Flatway?

VANE
Fleetway.

[**FLEETWAY** comes up.

FRUST
Mr Fleetway, I want to say I thought your Orphoos very remarkable. Fine.

FLEETWAY
Thank you, sir, indeed—so glad you liked it.

FRUST [A little balder in the eye]
There wasn't much to it, but what there was was fine. Mr Toone.

[**FLEETWAY** melts out and **TOONE** is precipitated.]

Mr Toone, I was very pleased with your Professor—quite a character-study. [**TOONE** bows and murmurs] Yes, sir! I thought it fine. [His eye grows bald] Who plays the goat?

MISS HOPKINS [Appearing suddenly between the windows]
I play the faun, Mr Frost.

FORESON [Introducing]
Miss Maude 'Opkins.

FRUST
Miss Hopkins, I guess your fawn was fine.

MISS HOPKINS
Oh! Thank you, Mr Frost. How nice of you to say so. I do so enjoy playing him.

FRUST
[His eye growing bald] Mr Foreson, I thought the way you fixed that tree was very cunning; I certainly did. Got a match?

[He takes a match from **FORESON**, and lighting a very long cigar, walks up Stage through the French windows followed by **FORESON**, and examines the apple-tree.]

[The two Actors depart, but Miss **HELLGROVE** runs from where she has been lingering, by the curtain, to **VANE**, Stage Right.]

MISS HELLGROVE
Oh! Mr Vane—do you think? He seemed quite—Oh! Mr Vane [ecstatically] If only—

VANE [Pleased and happy]
Yes, yes. All right—you were splendid. He liked it. He quite—

MISS HELLGROVE [Clasping her hand]
How wonderful Oh, Mr Vane, thank you!

[She clasps his hands; but suddenly, seeing that **FRUST** is coming back, fits across into the curtain and vanishes.

[The Stage, in the crude light, as empty now save for **FRUST**, who, in the French windows, Centre, is mumbling his cigar; and **VANE**, Stage Right, who is looking up into the wings, Stage Left.]

VANE [Calling up]
That lighting's just right now, Miller. Got it marked carefully?

ELECTRICS
Yes, Mr Vane.

VANE
Good. [To **FRUST** who as coming down] Well, sir? So glad—

FRUST
Mr Vane, we got little Miggs on contract?

VANE
Yes.

FRUST
Well, I liked that little pocket piece fine. But I'm blamed if I know what it's all about.

VANE [A little staggered]
Why! Of course it's a little allegory. The tragedy of civilization—all real feeling for Beauty and Nature kept out, or pent up even in the cultured.

FRUST
Ye-ep. [Meditatively] Little Miggs'd be fine in "Pop goes the Weasel."

VANE
Yes, he'd be all right, but—

FRUST
Get him on the 'phone, and put it into rehearsal right now.

VANE
What! But this piece—I—I—!

FRUST
Guess we can't take liberties with our public, Mr Vane. They want pep.

VANE [Distressed]
But it'll break that girl's heart. I—really—I can't—

FRUST
Give her the part of the 'tweeny in "Pop goes".

VANE
Mr Frust, I—I beg. I've taken a lot of trouble with this little play. It's good. It's that girl's chance—and I—

FRUST
We-ell! I certainly thought she was fine. Now, you 'phone up Miggs, and get right along with it. I've only one rule, sir! Give the Public what it wants; and what the Public wants is punch and go. They've got no use for Beauty, Allegory, all that high-brow racket. I know 'em as I know my hand.

[During this speech **MISS HELLGROVE** is seen listening by the French window, in distress, unnoticed by either of them.]

VANE
Mr Frost, the Public would take this, I'm sure they would; I'm convinced of it. You underrate them.

FRUST
Now, see here, Mr Blewitt Vane, is this my theatre? I tell you, I can't afford luxuries.

VANE
But it—it moved you, sir; I saw it. I was watching.

FRUST [With unmoved finality]
Mr Vane, I judge I'm not the average man. Before "Louisa Loses" the Public'll want a stimulant. "Pop goes the Weasel" will suit us fine. So—get right along with it. I'll go get some lunch.

[As he vanishes into the wings, Left, **MISS HELLGROVE** covers her face with her hands. A little sob escaping her attracts **VANE'S** attention. He takes a step towards her, but she flies.

VANE [Dashing his hands through his hair till it stands up]
Damnation!

[**FORESON** walks on from the wings, Right.

FORESON
Sir?

VANE
"Punch and go!" That superstition!

[**FORESON** walks straight out into the wings, Left.

VANE
Mr Foreson!

FORESON [Re-appearing]
Sir?

VANE
This is scrapped. [With savagery] Tell 'em to set the first act of "Louisa Loses," and put some pep into it.

[He goes out through the French windows with the wind still in his hair.

FORESON [In the centre of the Stage]
Electrics!

ELECTRICS
Hallo!

FORESON
Where's Charlie?

ELECTRICS
Gone to his dinner.

FORESON
Anybody on the curtain?

A VOICE
Yes, Mr Foreson.

FORESON
Put your curtain down.

[He stands in the centre of the Stage with eyes uplifted as the curtain descends.

John Galsworthy – A Short Biography

John Galsworthy, eldest son of John Galsworthy (1817-1904), a solicitor and company director of Old Jewry, London, and Blanche Bailey (1835-1915), daughter of Charles Bartleet, a needlemaker in Redditch. His father's ancestors originated in Wembury, near Plymouth in England, and Galsworthy, for whom family origins were of significant importance, maintained a close connection with Devon. His more immediate family were considerably wealthy and well established in the shipping industry, and owned a fine estate in Kingston-upon-Thames called Parkfield, where Galsworthy was born on the 14th August 1867. At the age of nine he began education at Saugeen, a Bournemouth preparatory school, before starting at Harrow school in 1881 where he remained until 1886, distinguishing himself as an athlete.

His education at Harrow being successful enough to gain him entrance to Oxford, he began at New College to read law and gained a second-class degree with honours in 1889. Following Lincoln's Inn he was called to the bar in 1890. Despite this recognition he realised that he was not keen to actually begin practising law and so he resolved instead to look after the family's shipping business while specialising himself in Marine Law. This decision saw him take to the seas to destinations such as Vancouver, Island and South AFrica, though it was at the age of twenty-five on one particular journey to Australia, motivated by an (unfulfilled) intention to meet Robert Louis Stevenson on Samoa that he would being to realise fully his literary interests: though he was not considering becoming a writer at this time, his enjoyment of literature was enough to encourage an attempt at meeting a great writer and eventually enabled one of the most significant encounters of his life. He made the journey with his friend Edward Sanderson and, though he missed Stevenson, he met Joseph Conrad, a fellow future author famed for his novels which were often nautically themed. At the time Conrad was the first mate of the sailing-ship Torrens moored in the harbour of Adelaide, Australia; still very much focused on his ship-borne career, he was yet to begin his writing in earnest.

Indeed, though neither knew at the time, both Conrad and Galsworthy were at similar junctures in their lives, their time spent as sea acting as a transitional period during which each found their literary calling. It is perhaps owning to this unknown common ground that they became close friends. During his time on the Torrens Galsworthy recorded several details, offering a frank and valuable characterisation of Conrad while also illuminating his own experiences as a student of Marine Law.

> "I supposed to be studying navigation for the Admiralty Bar, would every day work out the position of the ship with the captain. On one side of the saloon table we would sit and check our observations with those of Conrad, who from the other side of the table would look at us a little quizzically."

On his return to England and the cessation of his nautical voyaging, Galsworthy began an affair with the wife of his first cousin, Major Arthur John Galsworthy. Ada Nemesis Pearson Cooper (1864-1956), the daughter of Emanuel Copper, an obstetrician from Norwich, remained married to the Major for ten years and the affair remained secret for its duration. In order to conceal the affair they took considerable pains to avoid suspicion. One such tactic was to stay in a secluded farmhouse called Wingstone in the village on Manaton on Dartmoor, in Devon. In Galsworthy's decision to choose Devon as the location for their clandestine rendezvous we see evidence of Galsworthy's affection for the place of his father's origin. It was only when, in 1905, she divorced the Major that their affair became known following their marriage on 23rd September of that year.

Galsworthy now took to writing sometime after having met Conrad and his career began in earnest when, in 1897, his first work, From the Four Winds, a volume of short stories, was published under the pseudonym John Sinjohn. He succeeded this in 1898 with Jocelyn, his first novel, and then his second in 1900, Villa Rubein. In 1901 he published a second volume of short stories, A Man of Devon, which was the last of his work to be published under pseudonym. The first of his work to be published under his own name was The Island Pharisees in 1904, a novel of social observation, seasoned with flashes of satire and propaganda. His decision to write under his own name is arguably owing to the recent death of his father, either as a mark of respect to his name or because now he was able to publish freely without incurring the possibility of paternal disappointment at his choice of career. It also marked a shift in his professionalism; he had hitherto published with small, independent publishers, but The Island Pharisees was published by Heinemann, a far more established House and one with whom he remained for the duration of his writing career.

He arguably cemented his position and maturity as a writer when, in 1906, he saw the publication of both his first major play, The Silver Box, and the novel The Man of Property. Each was published to considerable critical acclaim, and to achieve both in such a short space of time was impressive. the Silver Box concerns the imbalance in the justice system with regards to criminals of differing class by contrasting the treatment of a poor thief and a rich thief, both of whom stole silver cigarette cases but for very different reasons. The complexity of individual experience when not dealt with in public is highlighted and questioned in a bravely critical manner; despite the clear issues it raises with class and privilege, the final night was attended by the Price and Princess of Wales. The Man of Property was the first novel in the famous The Forsyte Saga, a trilogy of novels with an 'interlude' between each one, written between 1906 and 1921. Dealing with the questions of status, class and materialism, The Man of Property introduces us to the Forsyte family, particularly Soames Forsyte, who is acutely aware of his status as 'new money' and equally keen to assert himself as a wealthy man. Jealous of his wife and desperate to own things in order to confirm his wealth to those observing him, he engineers a plan to keep his wife from her friends which backfires spectacularly when, instead of cutting her off, all Soames achieves is enabling her to have an affair. This drives Soames to terrible actions with terrible consequences, which Galsworthy depicts with confidence.

Very typically Edwardian, the novel focuses on conflict between property and art, and to a certain degree much of its emotional power is drawn from Galsworthy's own life, particularly his affair with Ada. Their rendezvous in the countryside of Devon mirror the manner in which Forsyte seeks to relocate his wife and; though theirs was a much healthier relationship, there are clear similarities. By examining the fragile nature of the class system and those moving within it Galsworthy offered an important perspective on the relationships between material wealth, personal happiness and obsession, and the manner in which these change over time. His contemporaries widely regarded the publication of this novel as marking the end of Victorianism. His friend Conrad praised it as "indubitably a piece of art" and, though the notoriously risqué D.H. Lawrence lamented the novel's timidity in the face of sexuality and sensuality, he considered it potentially "a very great novel, a very great satire".

Though he continued to write both plays and novels, it was his work as a playwright for which he was most celebrated by his contemporaries. Indeed, his next novel, The Country House, seems uncharacteristically unfocused, its satirical view of those belonging to the country set comparatively unremarkable and weakly characterised, while at times the tone of satire becomes one of ironic detachment. In 1909 he published Fraternity, an exploration of of the various connections between urban society and the social classes therein, though its representation of lower-class Londoners is utterly unconvincing and ill-informed. Remaining with the subject of the landed gentry and the society surrounding it, in 1915 he published The Freelands, which does not stray far from conservative discussions of capitalism, the rural economy and their interrelationship.

His drama, however, featured a convincingly muted realism, directed at a relatively small, educated and politically-aware audience. His social agenda is prevalent here too, and is represented in a simple and static manner producing arresting instances of high drama. This talent for creating moments of captivating theatre is complimented by an instinctual sense of balance enabling his narratives to vacillate between their emotional high- and low-points, ultimately reaching conclusive equilibrium. This is particularly evident in one of his most popular plays, Strife, published in 1909 and examining the antagonists in a strike at a Cornish tin mine. In this, and in 1910's Justice, he approaches his subject with sympathy, irony and balance, which establishes a position of narrative authority while garnering the audiences trust that he is representing his characters and their motives justly. Justice condemns the use of solitary confinement in prisons, a reformist agenda which caught the liberality of his contemporary audiences along with the home secretary, Winston Churchill. Despite he was careful to disassociate himself with politics and professed himself apolitical, he and his work were nevertheless aligned with the views of the Liberal establishment. He spent much of the duration of the First World War working in a field hospital in France as an orderly having been passed over for military service.

Despite the popularity and brilliance of his work, it was only in 1920 that he had his first true commercial success with The Skin Game, a melodrama dealing with ethics, property and class. The play was adapted by Alfred Hitchcock in 1931. Galsworthy, meanwhile, had turned down a knighthood in 1918, considering his work not sufficient to be made a knight of the realm. He did, however, accept the Belgian Palmes d'Or in the following year. In 1920 he published the second novel in the Forsyte Saga, In Chancery, in which he resumes many of the themes of the first novel, focusing on the marital disharmony between Soames Forsyte and his wife. Katherine Mansfield considered it "a fascinating, brilliant book" in her review in The Atheneum. Then, in 1921, he was elected as the PEN International Literary Club's first president. The concluding novel to The Forsyte Saga, To Let was published in 1921 with a kind of peace being found between Forsyte and his now-ex wife, though he is left contemplating his losses and his greed. More ironic treatment of class confusions followed in Loyalties, bringing with it more popular success which lasted until 1926 and Escape, the last of his popular plays. Though he enjoyed popular success it was inconsistent and relatively small. His Collected Plays was published in 1929.

Over the course of time the appreciation of his work has gradually shifted from his plays to his novels, and particularly the detail and intricacy of his chronicle of English social difference, tension and pretension in The Forsyte Saga. Its success encouraged Galsworthy to revisit Soames Forsyte in a second trilogy, A Modern Comedy, which follows Soames's obsessive love of his daughter Fleur. In its three volumes, The White Monkey (1924), The Silver Spoon (1936) and Swan Song (1928) he examines the English commercial upper-middle class and its ideologies, its instinct to possess as its only way of distinguishing itself manifested in the poisonous materialism of Soames. Interestingly, this emergent social class which he so vehemently criticises is the very class from which he emerged. He witnessed first-hand its insularity, its chauvinism, its restrictive and oppressive morality, its stubborn imperialism and its materialism, and it is this experience which enables him to write so comfortably about it. Swan Song is widely considered among the best of Galsworthy's writing for the depth of its exploration of society and its heightened emotional subtlety. In 1929 he was appointed to the Order of Merit, despite having turned down a knighthood earlier. He spent his last years writing a third trilogy, End of the Chapter, beginning in 1931 with Maid in Waiting, Flowering Wilderness in 1932 and concluding with Over The River in 1933. These are significantly less coherent works and are indicative of his deteriorating health. Indeed, in 1932 he was awarded the Nobel Prize, though he was too ill to attend the ceremony.

Throughout the course of his career he received honorary degrees from the universities of St Andrews (1922), Manchester (1927), Dublin (1929), Cambridge (1930), Sheffield (1930), Oxford (1931), and Princeton (1931). In 1926 New College, Oxford, elected him as an honourary fellow. In photographs he is portrayed as handsome, fastidiously dressed and dignified. He was unusually compassionate and this saw him involved in several charitable and humane causes throughout the course of his life, including penal reforms, attacks on theatrical censorship and campaigning for animal rights. Though he spent the majority of the final seven years of his life at his home in Bury, West Sussex, it was at his home in Hampstead, London, that he died of a brain tumour on 31st January, 1933, six weeks after having been too ill to attend the ceremony in honour of his receiving the Nobel Prize. According to demands made in his will he was cremated and his ashes scattered over the South Downs from an aeroplane. Also in his will was his wish to leave cottages to several of his astonished tenants. He is memorialised in Highgate 'New' Cemetery and in the cloisters of New College, Oxford, where he was an honourary fellow.

John Galsworthy – A Concise Bibliography

From the Four Winds, 1897 (as John Sinjohn)
Jocelyn, 1898 (as John Sinjohn)
Villa Rubein, 1900 (as John Sinjohn)
A Man of Devon, 1901 (as John Sinjohn)
The Island Pharisees, 1904
The Silver Box, 1906 (his first play)
The Man of Property, 1906 – First book of The Forsyte Saga (1922)
The Country House, 1907

A Commentary, 1908
Fraternity, 1909
A Justification for the Censorship of Plays, 1909
Strife, 1909
Fraternity, 1909
Joy, 1909
Justice, 1910
A Motley, 1910
The Spirit of Punishment, 1910
Horses in Mines, 1910
The Patrician, 1911
The Little Dream, 1911
The Pigeon, 1912
The Eldest Son, 1912
Quality, 1912
Moods, Songs, and Doggerels, 1912
For Love of Beasts, 1912
The Inn of Tranquillity, 1912
The Dark Flower, 1913
The Fugitive, 1913
The Mob, 1914
The Freelands, 1915
The Little Man, 1915
A Bit o' Love, 1915
A Sheaf, 1916
The Apple Tree, 1916
The Foundations, 1917
Beyond, 1917
Five Tales, 1918
Indian Summer of a Forsyte, 1918 – First interlude of The Forsyte Saga
Saint's Progress, 1919
Addresses in America, 1912
In Chancery, 1920 – Second book of The Forsyte Saga
Awakening, 1920 – Second interlude of The Forsyte Saga
The Skin Game, 1920
To Let, 1921 – Third book of The Forsyte Saga
A Family Man, 1922
The Little Man, 1922
Loyalties, 1922
Windows, 1922
Captures, 1923
Abracadabra, 1924
The Forest, 1924
Old English, 1924
The White Monkey, 1924 – First book of A Modern Comedy (1929)
The Show, 1925
Escape, 1926
The Silver Spoon, 1926 – Second book of A Modern Comedy

Verses New and Old, 1926

Castles in Spain, 1927

A Silent Wooing, 1927 – First Interlude of A Modern Comedy

Passers By, 1927 – Second Interlude of A Modern Comedy

Swan Song, 1928 – Third book of A Modern Comedy

The Manaton Edition, 1923–26 (collection, 30 vols.)

Exiled, 1929

The Roof, 1929

On Forsyte 'Change, 1930

Two Essays on Conrad, 1930

Soames and the Flag, 1930

The Creation of Character in Literature, 1931 (The Romanes Lecture for 1931).

Maid in Waiting, 1931 – First book of End of the Chapter (1934)

Forty Poems, 1932

Flowering Wilderness, 1932 – Second book of End of the Chapter

Autobiographical Letters of Galsworthy: A Correspondence with Frank Harris, 1933

One More River (originally Over the River), 1933 – Third book of End of the Chapter

The Grove Edition, 1927–34 (collection, 27 Vols.)

Collected Poems, 1934

Punch and Go, 1935

The Life and Letters, 1935

The Winter Garden, 1935

Forsytes, Pendyces and Others, 1935

Selected Short Stories, 1935

Glimpses and Reflections, 1937

Galsworthy's Letters to Leon Lion, 1968

Letters from John Galsworthy 1900–1932, 1970

Caravan the assembled tales of John Galsworthy, New York Charles Scribner's Sons 1925

www.ingramcontent.com/pod-product-compliance
Lightning Source LLC
Chambersburg PA
CBHW060117050426
42448CB00010B/1913